C000126431

STRANGERS AND NOMADS

Dedicated to the English and Welsh Martyrs

STRANGERS AND NOMADS

CATHOLIC MARTYRS OF ENGLAND AND WALES

DUDLEY PLUNKETT

Gracewing

First published in England in 2021
by
Gracewing
2 Southern Avenue
Leominster
Herefordshire HR6 0QF
United Kingdom
www.gracewing.co.uk

No part of this publication may be reproduced, stored in a
retrieval system, or transmitted in any form or by any means,
electronic, mechanical, photocopying, recording or otherwise,
without the written permission of the publisher.

The right of Dudley Plunkett to be identified
as the author of this work has been asserted in accordance
with the Copyright, Designs and Patents Act 1988.

© 2021 Dudley Plunkett

ISBN 978 085244 980 6

Nihil Obstat: Rev. William Wilson, Censor deputatis

Imprimatur: ✠ Rt. Rev. Philip A. Egan BA, STL, PhD
Bishop of Portsmouth
28 May 2021

The Nihil Obstat and Imprimatur are official declarations that a
book or pamphlet is free of doctrinal or moral error. No implica-
tion is contained therein that those who have granted the Nihil
Obstat and Imprimatur agree with the contents, opinions or
statements expressed.

Typeset by Gracewing

Cover design by Bernardita Peña Hurtado,
incorporating stained glass by Margaret Pope
in the Shrine of the Sacred Heart and the English Martyrs
at Tyburn Convent.

CONTENTS

FOREWORD

 EARS AGO, WHEN I was at school, we used to
hear a lot about 'The Martyrs', St John
Fisher and St Thomas More and the 284
canonised or beatified women and men who died
for the Catholic Faith during the Reformation. The
martyrs captured our imagination. They inspired
us. They were English or Welsh, so they seemed real,
despite the gap of history. These days, for some
reason, we do not hear as much about them. This is
a pity, because if we do not know our history, any
community, let alone the Catholic community, will
lose its bearings. True, as Catholics today we are not
persecuted so much for our beliefs specifically about
the Mass or the nature of the Church, but in a secular
culture we are often pilloried for other aspects of our
faith, and in particular for our 'anthropology', for
what it means to be human, and our convictions
about the inviolable dignity of human life from
conception to natural death. Pope St John Paul II
once said that 'when the sense of God is lost, there

is also a tendency to lose the sense of man, of his dignity and his life'[1] .

This is why I am delighted to commend to readers this new book by Dudley Plunkett. As he says in the Introduction, there are numerous books and pamphlets about the lives of the martyrs and their history, but relatively few that focus on devotion to them and the importance of seeking their intercession for our (urgent) spiritual needs today. In Part One, Dr Plunkett sets the scene in penal times before going on to speak of what the martyrs mean for us and the power of their prayer. In Part Two, he presents profiles of the canonised martyrs in date order, according to their feast-days, together with the Collect prayer from the Roman Missal and other sources. The profiles often recall poignant sayings of the martyrs and many testimonies to their bravery.

Strangers and Nomads will surely be an inspiration to us all to seek the intercession of these brave men and women, clergy and laity who have gone before us in the Faith. It will help us to become firmer in our faith in God and in what it means to be human. Tertullian, the early Christian apologist, once famously said: 'The blood of the martyrs is the seed of Christians.'[2] The testimony of the English and Welsh martyrs makes these lands of ours holy, a fertile ground for mission. I pray that this new book will help us all become more

---

[1]   Pope St John Paul II, *Evangelium Vitae*, 21.

[2]   Tertullian, *Apologeticus*, 13.

effective and more credible witnesses to Jesus Christ. In these difficult times, may the prayers and example of the martyrs help us to draw many more souls into the happiness and joy of full communion with Christ in His Church.

In Corde Iesu,

✠ Philip
Bishop of Portsmouth
4 May 2021, Feast of the English Martyrs

ACKNOWLEDGEMENTS

 OWE SPECIAL DEBTS of gratitude to the Sisters of the Community of the Benedictine Adorers of the Heart of Jesus, at Tyburn Convent, for their example, prayers and helpfulness, to Rev. Martin Plunkett, Parish Priest of St Thomas More, Eastcote, for many exploratory conversations and valuable insights, to Deacon Craig Aburn, Editor of the Portsmouth Diocesan e-News, who encouraged the first drafts of my research into the lives of the Forty Martyrs, and most especially to Bishop Philip Egan, for his Imprimatur and his generous Foreword.

INTRODUCTION

 HERE IS NO shortage of pamphlet-style publications about the Catholic martyrs of England and Wales during the Reformation and Penal Times and there are numerous books published about the most well-known amongst them. However, there are few works in which the story of their lives and sufferings have been gathered together with the deliberate intention of spreading devotion to them and encouraging seeking their intercession for the spiritual needs of contemporary society. In his thoroughly researched book, Malcolm Pullan[3] provides an invaluable source of information on the martyrs, but his is essentially a reference work that does not treat the martyrs primarily as intercessors. The English and Welsh martyrs of this period have been

---

[3] M. Pullan, *The Life and Times of the Forty Martyrs of England and Wales.*

largely relegated to the status of historical icons, most of them feted only on special occasions but rarely seen as individuals who can be asked to pray for the renewal of the Catholic faith in our times.

In my book on St Philip Howard,[4] I emphasised this aspect of the martyr's life and significance, and indeed, as co-patron of the English Diocese of Arundel and Brighton, he is more worthily commemorated than many of his companion martyrs. It was while researching for the book that I became aware of the apparent neglect of most of the martyrs by the contemporary Church which is so much in need of their help at a time of spiritual crisis. We are living in an age when the Church is afflicted with internal conflict and weakening of faith. It might be appropriate even to speak of a second Reformation, given the confusion that characterises Christian thinking today, with the difference that the original Reformation was largely theological and political in nature whereas today Christian faith is being undermined by a secular materialist culture.

Even with the harrowing experience of the coronavirus pandemic, there has been little evidence that people in the main turn to God to have a sense of where they are being led and what his will is for the world. While it is well and good to seek solutions in science, these need to be reviewed against any indications that God might have plans for a spiritual re-setting of contemporary faith and culture. Here is where the saints, and especially the

4 D. Plunkett, *The Noble Martyr.*

martyrs, have a role. They died willingly, not simply in obedience to God's will but in the hope that the Catholic faith would be restored in their country, and this intention is no less apposite today.

It cannot be denied that there is a lack of a supernatural perspective, of a sense of God as the foundation of all reality, in today's world. To think supernaturally is to see with God's vision, to sense his purpose in people, events, sufferings, joys, life, and death, to realise the immensity by which heavenly life surpasses earthly life. The supernatural can be absent from our consciousness even as Church as well as in the way we pose to ourselves the central issues of our time. Rationalism takes over, and the religious view can become conflated with the secular, being just a little more high-minded or apparently altruistic.

It is not the intention of this work to devalue the ecumenical efforts that have been made to bring closer together the Catholic Church and the ecclesiastical communities of the Reformation, or in any way to re-open old wounds of hostility or mistrust. However, Christian unity can only come through God's help and through a deeper appreciation of the true history involved. This perspective could lead to enlisting the martyrs' intercession for unity and for the healing that is needed through our repentance and God's mercy. It is therefore my hope, by evoking the lives and merits of the martyrs, to help reclaim their assistance in a rediscovery of spiritual wisdom, both within and outside the Church, that will bring about a renewed faith benefiting directly from the prayers of the '*strangers and nomads*' (Hebrews 11:13) who suffered and shed their blood for the truth and for the Eucharistic unity of Christians in their country.

REMEMBERING THE MARTYRS

N 25 OCTOBER 1970, Pope Paul VI canonised as martyrs forty people who had given their lives for their Catholic faith during the period when its practice was proscribed in England and Wales. He welcomed their canonisation in a prayerful homily:

> May the Lord grant us the grace that in these times of religious indifferentism and increasingly rampant theoretical and practical materialism, the example and intercession of the Holy Forty Martyrs comfort us in faith, strengthen our authentic love for God, for his Church, and for all men. May the blood of these Martyrs be able to heal the great wound inflicted upon God's Church by reason of the separation of the Anglican Church from the Catholic Church.

> Is it not one—these Martyrs say to us—the
> Church founded by Christ? Is not this their
> witness? Their devotion to their nation
> gives us the assurance that on the day
> when—God willing—the unity of the faith
> and of Christian life is restored, no offence
> will be inflicted on the honour and sover-
> eignty of a great country such as England.[1]

The forty were only a fraction of the faithful
Catholics who had suffered grievously or had been
executed under a corrupt judicial system or
through the unjust penal laws enacted by the
reigning monarchs, encouraged by Protestant
supporters and other upholders of the title of
Supreme Head of the Church in England claimed
by Henry VIII.

The English martyrs, both beatified and canonised, are commemorated in a feast-day on 4 May,
and a similar feast-day has been instituted for the
martyrs of Wales on 25 October. Many of these are
scarcely remembered individually but they can
nonetheless be invoked collectively for blessings
on their countries in a later time. This book
recounts the lives of the canonised martyrs of the
Reformation, that is the Forty Martyrs of England
and Wales and the three other saints martyred on
English soil who were separately canonised,
namely St Thomas More, St John Fisher, and St
Oliver Plunkett.

---

[1]   Pope St Paul VI, *Homily at the Canonisation of the Forty
      Martyrs* (25 October 1970).

The Penal Times

The description *Penal Times* is applied to a century and a half of English history when Catholicism was literally and effectively outlawed by a series of penal laws. These laws imposed severe financial penalties and imprisonment on practising Catholics and obliged them to attend the officially recognised church services and to take oaths recognising the authority of the Monarch over the Church in place of that of the Pope. They also specified as treasonous crimes ministering as a Catholic priest, returning to the country after being ordained abroad, and the possession of items of Catholic religious devotion. These measures were applied in England with varying rigour beginning in the reign of Henry VIII and lasting until the 1680s, when their injustice finally began to be recognised.

The events that marked these times, and which help explain the severity with which the penal laws operated, stemmed from the refusal of the Pope to grant Henry VIII an annulment or divorce from Catherine of Aragon, his wife of twenty-five years and the mother of his daughter, Mary. Frustrated by lengthy and unsuccessful negotiations with the Pope, Henry decided upon a sundering of the ties of the Church in England to papal authority and he assumed the title of Supreme Head of the Church in England. This action was confirmed by the Act of Supremacy (1534) and provided a pretext for the pillaging of Church possessions and the dissolution of the monasteries and religious houses, while the Treason Act (1534) made it punishable by death to deny the King his title by refusing to take the Oath of Supremacy.

Following the intermission of the reign of the Catholic Queen Mary (1553–1558), whose efforts to restore the Catholic faith were sometimes harsh and counter-productive, the legislative measures taken by Henry VIII were continued and reinforced under Edward VI with the Act of Uniformity (1549) which abolished the Mass and was then revised and renewed by Elizabeth I (1558–1603). A new Act of Supremacy (1558) confirmed the Queen as Supreme Governor of the Church in England and re-imposed the oath that required the swearing of allegiance to the Monarch under this title. The revised Act of Uniformity (1558) specified *The Book of Common Prayer* as the form for services in the official Church and required everyone to attend church each week or incur a fine. A further measure, the Supremacy of the Crown Act (1562), made it a crime of treason to persist in refusing to take the Oath of Supremacy.

In 1570, the papal bull *Regnans in Excelsis* of Pius V excommunicated Elizabeth I and absolved Catholics from their obedience to her. This launched decades of violent persecution, when the very identity of people as Catholics was enough for them to incur severe penalties, especially if they were priests. A series of legal measures was enacted, making it an act of treason to declare the Queen a heretic or to reconcile any person to the Catholic Church, and depriving people of their property if found bringing into the country Catholic religious articles, such as *Agnus Dei* medallions, rosaries, or books. Celebrating or assisting at Mass was prohibited, subject to substantial fines and imprisonment for priests, and there were fines for not attending official Church services. Specific measures were enacted against priests, who were required to leave the country or else face the charge of high treason, and penalties of fines or imprisonment were imposed for harbouring or assisting priests.

A series of ineffectual conspiracies, by Ridolfi (1571), Throckmorton (1583), and Babington (1586), aimed at de-throning Elizabeth, stirred up anti-Catholic hatred and recriminations. The Spanish Armada (1588) ignited further anti-Catholic sentiment, and Catholics who could in any way be suspected of supporting the intended invasion were rounded up and imprisoned. There followed the Gunpowder Plot (1604) against James I, which led to the deaths of several conspirators. Much later, the fictitious Popish Plot (1678), supposedly against Charles II but which was invented by Titus Oates, led to the deaths of at least twenty-three innocent Catholics, including six of the Forty Martyrs.

From the latter years of the 18th century, legislation repealing the penal measures was gradually introduced, culminating in the Catholic Emancipation Act (1829) which ensured much greater freedom from discrimination for Catholics, even though some anti-Catholic laws have persisted to the present time, such as that which disqualifies

Catholics from the place they would otherwise occupy in the line of succession to the throne.

THE IMPORTANCE OF THE MARTYRS

Christian martyrs are men and women who in their lives bore witness to Christ and his Gospel to the point of dying at the hands of their adversaries. The Forty Martyrs represented a cross-section of secular and religious priests, and lay men and women, many of whom, such as Edmund Campion and Robert Southwell, were gifted scholars, poets, writers, or people of outstanding virtue and courage like Henry Morse, who in other circumstances might have graced the culture of their times. It is noteworthy that these three were Jesuits whose lives have been remembered and celebrated by their Order, while many others have remained in relative obscurity. Although not the first to be martyred by Henry VIII, Thomas More and Bishop John Fisher were canonised in 1935, thirty-five years before the Forty Martyrs, while the Irish Primate, Archbishop Oliver Plunkett, the last martyr to be executed on the Tyburn Tree[2] in

---

[2] The Tyburn Tree, near Marble Arch, London, was constructed of three cross-pieces, fastened in a triangle, and supported on three uprights. Nooses were tied to the crossbeams, and the person to be hanged was driven in a cart under one of the nooses. When it had been fastened round his or her throat, the cart was driven away. As many as twenty corpses could be left hanging there on the same day. A plaque on an adjacent wall records that '105 Catholic martyrs lost their lives at the Tyburn gallows near this site 1535–1681'.

1681, was canonised in 1975. These three saints cannot be omitted from the scope of this work because they had a major impact on the Church and society both of their times and since.

In addition to those canonised, no less than 242 further Catholic martyrs who died in England, Wales, Scotland, and Ireland were beatified by Popes Leo XIII, Pius XI and St John Paul II.[3] When, in 1987, Pope St John Paul II beatified eighty-five of them, he paid tribute to them in his homily at the beatification ceremony, affirming that they 'consciously and willingly embraced death for love of Christ and the Church':

> Among these eighty-five martyrs we find priests and laymen, scholars and craftsmen … What unites them all is the sacrifice of their lives in the service of Christ their Lord. The priests among them wished only to feed their people with the Bread of Life and with the Word of the Gospel. To do so meant risking their lives. But for them this price was small compared to the riches they could bring to their people in the Holy Sacrifice of the Mass … Laymen and priests worked together; together they stood on the scaffold and together welcomed death … They have earned our undying admiration and remembrance.[4]

---

[3]   See the Appendix for a list of the 242 beatified martyrs.
[4]   Pope St John Paul, *Homily at the Beatification of the Eighty-five martyrs of England, Wales, Scotland, and Ireland* (22 November 1987).

These martyrs are of greater significance than has generally been acknowledged, albeit that some have been formally honoured as the patrons of parish churches and schools. To ignore or forget them is all the more unjust when we reflect that they represent an even greater number of faithful Catholic recusants[5] and others who shared their spirit and their sufferings even if they were not put to death. Many of these endured far longer imprisonment than the martyrs, and in equally bad conditions that often led to their deaths. Alice Wells, the wife of the martyr St Swithun Wells, who was found guilty with her husband of harbouring priests, was consigned to prison until her death ten years later. Francis Tregian was deprived of all his possessions and imprisoned for 28 years for protecting another martyr, St Cuthbert Mayne, but was then released into exile in 1605 and died in Lisbon in 1608. How many others there were like this we do not know, but they are all important because they willingly suffered for the Catholic faith in England and Wales and should justly be reclaimed as intercessors for the spiritual revival of Catholicism in their country.

It therefore tells us something that the fiftieth anniversary of the canonisation of the Forty Martyrs passed in 2020 without any fanfare and that, although a number of individual martyrs, such as St John Southworth in Westminster or St Philip Howard in Arundel and Brighton, figure in

---

[5]   Faithful Catholics who refused to attend services of the official Church during the Penal Times.

diocesan calendars, few of their feast-days feature in the National Liturgical Calendars. Exceptions are the three martyr saints canonised separately from the Forty Martyrs, the three women martyrs, Anne Line, Margaret Ward, and Margaret Clitherow, and the six Welsh martyrs. Thus, none of the feast-days of the English priests among the Forty Martyrs, whether seminary priests or members of religious orders, or of the five English laymen, is included in the National Liturgical Calendar. This disregard surely betokens a lack of appreciation for those who gave their lives for the preservation of the Catholic faith and the Mass in England during the Penal Times.

THEIR BACKGROUNDS AND FATE

The Forty Martyrs came from twenty-six English and Welsh counties. Half of them were under forty years of age when they died; indeed, some hardly had time to exercise their priestly functions on their return to England after ordination. The youngest, Edmund Gennings, was executed when he was only twenty-four. Few of the forty reached the age of sixty and only one, John Kemble, who was eighty when he was brought to the scaffold, reached old age. They came from seven different religious Orders, nine of them Jesuits, thirteen being secular priests, and included eight lay persons, of whom three were women.

The priests, most often newly ordained abroad, returned to their country knowing that they might only survive for a matter of weeks or months at best. We need to heed the evidence of their physical and mental suffering to appreciate their sacrifice and the strength of their faith. Their lives were hard, full of every kind of discomfort, deprivation, and threat. They endured persecution, being hunted by the *poursuivants* (priest-hunters), having no fixed abode. Many of them endured days in hiding, confined in cupboard-like structures, or priests' holes, to escape men seeking financial reward for their capture. Under the penal laws, they became *strangers and nomads* in their own country. Their deaths were a public spectacle, answering to the curiosity of crowds avid for gruesome entertainment. Eighteen of the Forty Martyrs were executed at Tyburn; others suffered in the locality from which they came or were arrested, apart from Nicholas Owen, who died on the rack in the Tower of London, and Philip Howard, who also died in the Tower after a long imprisonment and possible poisoning.

The martyrs were confined in overcrowded, foul, and verminous conditions, often on starvation rations, cold, in dungeons that could be subject to flooding, and the victims of their jailers' profiteering if they sought better bedding or food. In addition to the agony of their execution by hanging and disembowelling, often while still conscious, most of them suffered torture in prison through the rack, the thumbscrew, the scavenger's daughter,[6] or by being suspended by their hands with toes just touching the floor for hours on end. Their torturers aimed at discovering information about their associates or obtaining confessions to crimes of treason. However, the more they were tortured, the more the martyrs seemed to find the strength to persevere without compromise in their faith and courage. The similarities between the martyrs' lives are evidence of their union of life and prayer, of the faith that motivated them, and of the holiness that bound them to God's will however sacrificial this may have been for them.

What do They Represent for Us?

The martyrs had the faith to accept unjust execution. We can admire their integrity in their refusal to take the Oath of Supremacy. Their final words that have been passed down to us speak not of misery and suffering but of undying hope, often despite long periods of mistreatment. They did not reckon the cost, as evidenced by their speeches at

---

6   The 'scavenger's daughter', named after a version of the name of Skevington, a Lieutenant of the Tower who introduced it, was a broad hoop of iron in two parts, fastened to each other by a hinge. The prisoner was made to kneel and to contract himself into a ball as far as he could. Then the torturer having placed the hoop under the victim's legs, knelt on his shoulders, to compress his body until the ends of the hoop could be fastened over the small of the back. After over an hour or more of such compression, blood emerged from the nostrils and even from the extremities of the hands and feet.

their trials and at the gallows. They fully exemplify
the prophetic words of Jesus:

> You will be dragged before governors and
> kings because of me, as a testimony to them
> and the Gentiles. When they hand you over,
> do not worry about how you are to speak or
> what you are to say; for what you are to say
> will be given to you at that time; for it is not
> you who speak, but the Spirit of your Father
> speaking through you. (Matthew 10:18–20)

In imitation of Jesus, they were able to forgive the
injustice of false accusations, persecution, cruel
torture, and the taking of their lives. They shared
an extraordinary love for the Holy Eucharist, and
it was this that they primarily sought to bring to
their fellow countrymen. They also had an
unshakeable commitment to the unity of the
Catholic Church under the Pope and a devotion
to the Blessed Mother of God, the Queen of Martyrs, whose shrines had been so desecrated.

The Holy Spirit spoke the truth through their
lives and the purity of their final declarations and
prayers, as will be recounted below. They were
people able to tell truth from falsehood who were
willing to lay down their lives out of love for God
and their faith. They are therefore a shining
example of true commitment and fidelity to the
Gospel, people who have given everything to God
in the faith and hope that their sacrifice would not
be in vain but for God's glory, for his will, and for
their salvation. They were people sustained by

prayer and graced by God to endure mental and bodily pain without complaint at all their afflictions, for they identified with Christ crucified. The martyrs showed this courage in the face of all threats and sufferings, going to greet death humbly, joyfully, and expressing their trust in God for eternal life. The bravery of the women martyrs is especially moving in their lack of regret for the help they gave to priests, and their willingness to undergo the vilest of deaths. Margaret Clitherow heroically refused to plead, so as to protect her family from having to give evidence at her trial, even under the threat of being pressed to death under a door weighted with stones while very possibly pregnant. The martyrs could not have been so fearless except as a work of grace.

THE POWER OF THEIR PRAYERS

We can well ask why did these people, who were innocent of any crime that could reasonably be attributed to them, arouse such animosity, deliberate injustice, and intense cruelty? If their country failed to recognise their virtues and sacrifices, it is certain that God can be trusted to do so, the more especially if they are celebrated by our seeking their intercession. The martyrs have received the reward of eternal life, and yet are still waiting for the answer to their pleas for the return of their country to the Catholic faith. The merits and prayers of such a formidable *cloud of witnesses* (Hebrews 12:1) are a treasury of potential blessings for the liberty and exaltation of the Church in modern times through repentance, conversions, and the restoration of the old faith without internal theological and moral divisions or external ideological hostility and threats from legislators, the media, and the culture of death present in abortion, euthanasia, and eugenics.

We can pray to them that, through their prayers, there can be reconciliation between Catholics and Protestants, for a true martyr considers no one their enemy. Although the martyrs are powerful in intercession, we do need to invoke them and to ask God to hear their prayers and ours, looking to how their lives and deaths can further God's plans for our times. We can seek the martyrs' intercession, for example, by celebrating their feast-days, by offering to them special intentions for prayer, by forming their names into a litany,[7] by choosing an individual martyr for special devotion, and by imitating their fidelity to the Church and their commitment to God's call.

If we ask ourselves what makes the difference between the challenges the martyrs faced in the society of their time and those we face today, it is certain that their challenges were much greater, so why is our response so much weaker? Does this not betray the poverty of the faith of our times and

---

[7]   See, for example, Catholic National Shrine and Basilica of Our Lady, *Litany of the Saints and Martyrs of England and Wales* (Walsingham, 2020), for a Litany of the Saints and Martyrs of England and Wales that includes many of the Blesseds.

how much we need spiritual purification and renewal? Are the martyrs not authentic guides to what God is asking of us, and can we not confidently count on their prayers of intercession and support? We can ask them to pray that God grants the blessing of new saints and inspired leaders and witnesses for the faith in what has become a nearly godless society. The martyrs are an example of hope and trust in God for those Christians who see the needy state of today's world and who, even if limited in what they can contribute practically, can also offer their prayers. From their heavenly vantage-point, the martyrs can better see the spiritual war that is being waged and are surely ready to give battle on behalf of the Church today against the forces of spiritual and moral evil.

RECLAIMING THE MARTYRS

The details of the martyrs' lives are gems to inspire prayers and thanks to God, and the Church has preserved the memory of many of them in relics, feasts, shrines and patronage of dioceses and churches. The Community of the Benedictine Adorers of the Heart of Jesus, a religious Order originating at the Basilica of the Sacré Coeur in Paris, has led the way in focusing attention on and devotion to the martyrs in the sure hope of their intercession for England. The Martyrs' Shrine at Tyburn, established by the French nuns at the suggestion of Cardinal Vaughan of Westminster in 1901, holds relics of many of the martyrs as well as a reconstruction of the Tyburn Tree on which they met their deaths. The 'Tyburn Nuns', as they have come to be called, remind us of how vital the memory of the English martyrs is for the Church in our times; they stand as both our treasure and our hope.

The Tyburn nuns have understood their vocation as praying perpetually before the Blessed Sacrament to intercede for the Church and for all God's people. At the same time, their vocation has given them an insight into the importance of those martyred for the Catholic faith in these lands. Their mission is twofold: keeping alive the memory of the heroic offering made by the martyrs whilst also enlisting their intercessory prayers for the fruitfulness of the Church today. They help us to see that the martyrs did not die in order to be remembered or considered as heroes, but so that the Catholic Church which they loved would continue to be the instrument of salvation for the world. These sisters can therefore be of great help to us in understanding how to enlist the witness and help of the martyrs for the spiritual needs of our time.

The lack of appreciation for the relevance of Catholicism to modern society is the result of the banishing of the Catholic way of life from England's history from the Reformation onwards. Therefore, reaching back to that time and reclaiming the faith for which the martyrs died implies both an historical *ressourcement* and a contemporary concern for an *aggiornamento*, to employ two major concepts that featured in the rationale for the Second Vatican Council. What is sought in reclaiming the martyrs' witness and intercession is not a return to the past but a reconnection so as to see current spiritual issues as part of the historical reality of the Catholic faith.

Encouragement can be drawn from the English and Welsh Bishops' initiative in 2020 to rededicate England to the Blessed Virgin Mary under the medieval title of *Our Lady's Dowry*. This unique designation grew largely from the devotion to Our Lady that had been inspired by the shrine of the Mother of God in Walsingham, Norfolk. Indeed, the desecration of Walsingham, among many other shrines, is one of the great tragedies and losses of the Penal Times. The subsequent obscuring of the Catholic understanding of the role of Our Lady in salvation history has had a detrimental effect on the vitality of the Catholic faith. A significant and providential sign of hope can therefore be seen in the Bishops' inspiration.

We can identify three elements of the pre-Reformation Church that were particularly significant for the martyrs, and which became targets for the Reformers: fidelity to the Pope and to the apostolic succession; the centrality of the Mass and the importance of the Holy Eucharist at the heart of the Church; and the communion with the saints in heaven, especially with Mary, the Mother of God. A reclaiming of the martyrs is therefore best understood as a desire to bring about a renewed commitment to these components of Catholic faith and practice and to their place in the evangelising of contemporary culture.

Attachment to the martyrs is sometimes associated with a 'traditionalist' religious stance, and devotion to them is perceived as aligned with a Catholic faith that seeks a restoration of a pre-Reformation mode of Catholicism. Whilst not wanting to impugn this understanding, I would suggest that a reclaiming of the martyrs would be hoping for something more. While much that has been part of Catholic history needs to be conserved and incorporated into the ongoing development of doctrine and practice of the faith, it is from the vantage point of the contemporary Church and culture that appeals for heaven's help need to be made.

PROFILES OF THE CANONISED MARTYRS

 HE FOLLOWING PROFILES of the Canonised Martyrs are arranged in date order of their feast-days.[1] The final words of the martyrs are quoted, where known, since these convey to us the state of mind and soul of those who are in the very act of surrendering their lives to execution. Furthermore, to underline the importance of having recourse to the martyrs' prayers for the restoration of the Catholic faith to their country, the Collects, or opening prayers of the Masses of their personal feast-days, are also given.

---

[1] Also included are the three separately canonised saints who died at Tyburn and the feast-days of groups of martyrs of England and Wales.

21 JANUARY

Bartholomew (later, Alban) Roe OSB (1583–1642)

Bartholomew was born in Suffolk and raised as a fervent Protestant. He attended Cambridge University and was converted to the Catholic faith in 1607 in his attempt to convert an imprisoned recusant. He began studies for the priesthood the following year at the English College at Douai, France, but sought admission to the Benedictine Order in 1612, taking the name Alban at his profession. He was associated with the monastery that eventually became Ampleforth Abbey, of which he is co-patron.

He served on the mission in England for three years after ordination. He was arrested, imprisoned for five years and then banished, but he returned to England for a further two years before being arrested again, after which he spent fifteen years in the Fleet prison. During this time, he was frequently released on day parole under oath to return at night, which enabled him to minister to recusants in London. However, during the severely anti-Catholic Long Parliament he was transferred to Newgate prison and was tried at the Old Bailey in 1642 for being a priest. When he was sentenced to be hanged, drawn, and quartered,[2]

---

[2]   This was the fate of all but a few of the martyrs, and consisted in being hanged, cut down often still alive, their genitals cut off, their stomachs ripped open, and

Alban thanked the judge with a low bow and said, 'How little this is in comparison to the bitter death which Christ suffered for me'. He was executed at Tyburn, on 21 January 1642, showing jocularity in remarks made to several people, including his executioner, but also protesting,

> See then, what the crime is for which I am to die, and whether my religion be my only treason … I wish I had a thousand lives then I would sacrifice them all for so worthy a cause.

Collect (for one martyr)

Almighty, ever-living God. By whose gift blessed Alban fought for righteousness's sake even until death, grant, we pray, through his intercession, that we may bear every adversity for the sake of your love and hasten with all our strength towards you who alone are life. Through our Lord, Jesus Christ, your Son, who lives and reigns with you in the unity of the Holy Spirit, God, for ever and ever. Amen.

St Alban, pray for us.

---

their heart and inner organs removed, their heads cut off, and their bodies cut into four pieces.

1 FEBRUARY

Henry Morse SJ (1595–1645)

ENRY MORSE WAS born in Suffolk and followed an extraordinarily adventurous career as a Catholic priest during the reign of Charles I and the Cromwellian revolution. Converted in his teenage years, he began studies for the priesthood at Douai at the age of 19. He returned to England but was arrested and imprisoned for four years and then banished as part of an amnesty granted to a hundred priests by King James I in 1618. He continued his studies at the English College in Rome, was ordained and requested entry into the Society of Jesus. He returned to England in 1624 where he joined the Jesuit novitiate and, after ministering in Northumberland for two years, was again arrested and imprisoned for three years in York Castle, where he completed the 30-day Ignatian retreat as part of the Jesuit novitiate and brought about the conversion of several of those imprisoned with him. Despite being banished in perpetuity, he returned to England in 1633 and was assigned to work in central London.

During the plague in 1635 he laboured hard among victims in London together with the future martyr John Southworth. He caught the plague himself but recovered from it. He was denounced as a priest and brought to trial, convicted, and imprisoned at Newgate in 1636. Thereafter, released from prison through the intervention of the King, and banished, he worked as a military chaplain in Flanders, but again, in 1643, returned to England where he ministered to recusants in various parts of the country before being finally arrested, imprisoned at Newgate, and condemned to death on the strength of his 1636 conviction. He was hanged, drawn, and quartered at Tyburn, on 1 February 1645. When at the scaffold he revealed that he had a secret to declare, the crowd grew silent, and he said,

> Gentlemen, take notice, the kingdom of England will never be truly blessed until it returns to the Catholic and apostolic faith... This is the secret ... this is the treason that I have to disclose.

Collect (Jesuit Missal and Lectionary)

Almighty, eternal God, you chose from the people of England and Wales St Henry to be made like Christ, who died to save the world. Listen to his prayers: strengthen the Church by the same faith and love that strengthened him and bless it always with your gift of unity. Through our Lord, Jesus Christ, your Son, who lives and reigns with you in the unity of the Holy Spirit, God, for ever and ever. Amen.

St Henry, pray for us.

21 FEBRUARY

Robert Southwell SJ (1561–1595)

OBERT, BORN IN Norfolk, joined the Jesuits in Rome at the age of 17 and was ordained a priest six years later. In 1586 he arrived in London with another priest, Henry Garnet, who was later martyred. For two years he travelled about the country on the Jesuit mission, several times narrowly escaping capture until, with the increase in persecution of Catholics suspected of assisting the Armada, he lodged for greater security at Arundel House, the home of Anne Howard, the wife of Philip Howard. Philip, Earl of Arundel, had been found guilty of treason for his Catholicism and had been imprisoned in the Tower of London. For the following six years Robert served the spiritual needs of Anne's household and ministered to many other Catholics both in London and in the surrounding counties. He also spent time writing works of poetry that have survived to this day, works which have been compared to the greatest, and indeed were admired by William Shakespeare.

Robert's presence in Arundel House was betrayed by a woman he had trusted and sought to help, and he was arrested on 25 June 1592, by Richard Topcliffe, the infamous priest-hunter, who held him prisoner and tortured him, with the consent of the Queen, to elicit information from him about those with whom he was associated, including Anne Howard. Eventually he was consigned to solitary confinement in the Tower, where he remained for nearly three years. Robert had befriended Philip Howard through a substantial correspondence while living in his wife's household and, although they never met in the Tower, they are known to have been aware of each other's presence. Robert was brought to trial on 20 February 1595 and condemned for being a priest. He was hanged, drawn, and quartered at Tyburn the following day.

In a speech at the scaffold, he concluded,

> And as to the Queen, I never attempted, nor contrived, or imagined any evil against her; but have always prayed for her to our Lord; and for this short time of my life still pray, that, in his infinite mercy, he would be pleased to give her all such gifts and graces, which he sees, in his divine wisdom, to be most expedient for the welfare, both of her soul and body, in this life and in the next. I commend, in like manner, to the same mercy of God, my poor country, and I implore the divine bounty to favour it with his light, and the knowledge of his truth, to the greater advancement of the salvation of souls, and the eternal glory of his divine Majesty. In fine, I beg of the Almighty and everlasting God, that this, my death, may be for my own and for my country's good, and the comfort of the Catholics my brethren.

Robert Southwell's most well-known poem is *The Burning Babe*:

As I in hoary winter's night stood shivering- in the snow,
Surprised I was with sudden heat which made my heart to glow;
And lifting up a fearful eye to view what fire was near,
A pretty babe all burning bright did in the air appear,
Who scorched with exceeding heat such floods of tears did shed,
As though His floods should quench His flames with what His tears were fed;
Alas! quoth He, but newly born in fiery heats of fry,
Yet none approach to warm their hearts or feel my fire but I!
My faultless breast the furnace is, the fuel wounding thorns;
Love is the fire and sighs the smoke, the ashes shame and scorns;
The fuel Justice layeth on, and Mercy blows the coals;
The metal in this furnace wrought are men's defiled souls;
For which, as now on fire I am, to work them to their good,
So will I melt into a bath, to wash them in my blood:
With this He vanish'd out of sight, and swiftly shrunk away.
And straight I called unto mind that it was Christmas-day.

Collect (Jesuit Missal and Lectionary)

Almighty, eternal God, you chose from the people of England and Wales St Robert to be made like Christ, who died to save the world. Listen to his prayers: strengthen the Church by the same faith and love that strengthened him, and bless it always with your gift of unity. Through our Lord, Jesus Christ, your Son, who lives and reigns with you in the unity of the Holy Spirit, God, for ever and ever. Amen.

St Robert, pray for us.

22 March

Nicholas Owen SJ (c.1550–1606)

 orn in Oxford into a Catholic family that gave several priests to the Church, Nicholas is outstanding even among the Forty Martyrs. Known for his skill as a carpenter, a craft he inherited from his father, and for his small size, he was responsible for the construction, during some twenty-six years, of a large number of marvellously ingenious hiding places (the famous *priests' holes*) which saved the lives of many priests in Catholic houses around the country during the Elizabethan persecution. These priests' holes were built into walls and chimney breasts, between floors, and under staircases, some only being discovered in the nineteenth and twentieth centuries. Nicholas, who had become a Jesuit lay brother, also helped Fr John Gerard SJ make his celebrated and unique escape from the Tower of London. In a hunt for priests in 1606, at Hindlip Hall, Worcestershire, Nicholas emerged from hiding, hoping in vain to avert the capture of Fr Henry Garnet SJ, the Jesuit Provincial, who was concealed in the same house. Despite merciless torture in the Tower, Nicholas uttered nothing but the words 'Jesus' and 'Mary' and gave no information to the authorities. Although he should have been exempt from torture because he had a serious hernia, his stomach split open while he was being stretched on the rack[3] and he died in agony on around 2 February 1606.

Collect (Jesuit Missal and Lectionary)

Almighty, eternal God, you chose from the people of England and Wales St Nicholas to be made like Christ, who died to save the world. Listen to his prayers: strengthen the Church by the same faith and love that strengthened him, and bless it always with your gift of unity. Through our Lord, Jesus Christ, your Son, who lives and reigns with you in the unity of the Holy Spirit, God, for ever and ever. Amen.

St Nicholas, pray for us.

---

[3]   The 'rack' was a torture practised in the Tower of London, in which the victim was attached hands and feet to a frame and then stretched by being winched, usually until limbs were dislocated. This torture was often repeated, in some known cases as many as ten times.

2 APRIL

John Paine (c. 1550–1582)

HOUGH LITTLE IS known of his early life, John was born in Peterborough. He was a convert, entered the English College at Douai in 1574, and was ordained two years later. He then returned to England with another future martyr, Cuthbert Mayne, and lived during his missionary life with the Petre family at Ingatestone House, in Essex, posing as an estate steward while ministering to the family and Catholics in the surrounding area.[4] He was arrested in 1581, racked in the Tower, and sentenced to death after false evidence had been brought against him (and indeed bought, at the price of £100) for conspiracy against the Queen. At his trial he protested that he was not guilty of any treason against the Queen and that men could not be made traitors just because they were ordained priests. He was executed by being hanged, drawn, and quartered on 2 April 1582 at Chelmsford.

---

[4]   In 1855 a priest's hiding-place was discovered at Ingatestone. The entrance to this secret chamber is from a small room attached to what was probably the host's bedroom. In the southeast corner the boards were found to be decayed; upon their removal, another layer of loose boards was observed to cover a hole or trapdoor, two feet square, with a ladder for access. The hiding-place measured fourteen feet in length, two feet one inch in breadth, and ten feet in height.

Before dying, he simply said,

> If it please the Queen and her Council that
> I shall die, I refer my case to God.

Collect

Almighty and merciful God, who brought your martyr blessed John to overcome the torments of his passion, grant that we, who celebrate the day of his triumph, may remain invincible under your protection against the snares of the enemy. Through our Lord, Jesus Christ, your Son, who lives and reigns with you in the unity of the Holy Spirit, God, for ever and ever. Amen.

St John, pray for us.

7 April

Henry Walpole SJ (1558–1595)

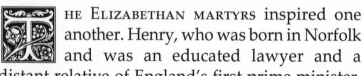 HE ELIZABETHAN MARTYRS inspired one another. Henry, who was born in Norfolk and was an educated lawyer and a distant relative of England's first prime minister, was not the only person who was moved to conversion at the execution of Edmund Campion in 1581 at Tyburn, where he was spattered by Edmund's blood. Though risking being found guilty of high treason if ordained abroad, he went to Douai, then joined the Jesuits in Rome, and filled posts in Italy, Spain, and Flanders during the course of several years before returning to England in December 1593. Unhappily, he was arrested and imprisoned the day after he landed. Over the next sixteen months he repeatedly suffered brutal torture. This was to avoid his dying on the rack. His hands were crippled by thumbscrews, but he gave nothing away. When he was brought to trial, the judges demanded he take the Oath of Supremacy acknowledging the Queen's authority in religion. He refused, was convicted, and hanged, drawn, and quartered in York on 7th April 1595.

At his trial Henry said,

> [Y]ou, my lords, sit here at present in judgment as men, and judge as such, being subject to error and passion; but know for certain, that there is a sovereign judge, who will judge righteously; whom in all things

we must obey in the first place; and then our lawful princes, in such things as are lawful, and no further.

Henry was also a gifted poet who wrote of the martyrs:

Whose patience rare and most courageous mind,
With fame renowned perpetual shall endure,
By whose examples we may rightly find,
Of holy life and death a pattern pure.
That we therefore their virtues may embrace
Pray we to Christ to guide us with his grace.

Collect (Jesuit Missal and Lectionary)

Almighty, eternal God, you chose from the people of England and Wales St Henry and companions to be made like Christ, who died to save the world. Listen to their prayers: strengthen the Church by the same faith and love that strengthened them, and bless it always with your gift of unity. Through our Lord, Jesus Christ, your Son, who lives and reigns with you in the unity of the Holy Spirit, God, for ever and ever. Amen.

St Henry, pray for us.

4 MAY

John Houghton OCart (c.1486–1535)

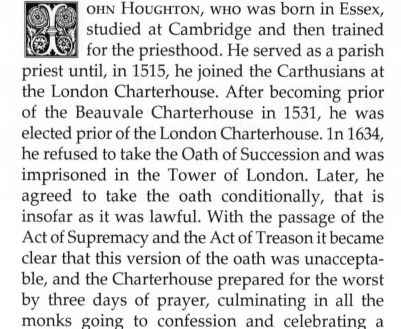

OHN HOUGHTON, WHO was born in Essex, studied at Cambridge and then trained for the priesthood. He served as a parish priest until, in 1515, he joined the Carthusians at the London Charterhouse. After becoming prior of the Beauvale Charterhouse in 1531, he was elected prior of the London Charterhouse. 1n 1634, he refused to take the Oath of Succession and was imprisoned in the Tower of London. Later, he agreed to take the oath conditionally, that is insofar as it was lawful. With the passage of the Act of Supremacy and the Act of Treason it became clear that this version of the oath was unacceptable, and the Charterhouse prepared for the worst by three days of prayer, culminating in all the monks going to confession and celebrating a votive Mass of the Holy Spirit.

Appearing before Cromwell, who was the lay Ecclesiastical Vicar General, John Houghton, together with two other Carthusian priors, had their oath with the stipulation, 'as far as the law of God allows', refused and they were sent to the Tower. At their trial, the jury was reluctant to declare such holy men guilty until their own lives were threatened by Cromwell. On 4 May 1535, the three Charterhouse monks were the first of the Forty Martyrs to be dragged on hurdles through the streets to Tyburn to be hanged, drawn, and quartered. John Houghton is recognised as the protomartyr of the English Reformation

In a final speech at the gallows, with the rope already around his neck, John said,

> I declare publicly that I refuse to comply with the will of our Lord the King, not out of any pertinacity, malice, or rebellious disposition, but only from the fear of God, lest I should offend His Sovereign Majesty, seeing our holy Mother the Church has decreed and determined otherwise than the King and his Parliament has ordained; wherefore I am obliged, in conscience, and am also ready and not dismayed, to suffer these and all possible torments rather than oppose the teaching of the Church.

St John, pray for us.

4 May

Robert Lawrence OCart (d.1535)

 OBERT, WHO IS believed to have come from Dorset, became a member of the Carthusian community at the London Charterhouse and was later prior of Beauvale. With Augustine Webster, he came to visit John Houghton to discuss their response to Henry VIII's religious policies, including the obligation to swear the Oath of Supremacy. The priors visited Thomas Cromwell and refused to take the Oath in the required form. Robert was reported at the interrogation as saying that there is one Catholic Church of which the Bishop of Rome is the head; therefore, he cannot believe that the King is supreme head of the Church. The three Carthusian priors were imprisoned in the Tower of London and executed for treason on 4 May 1535. Thomas More, himself a prisoner in the Tower, watched them leave on their way to Tyburn just weeks before Bishop John Fisher and himself were to suffer beheading.

St Robert, pray for us.

Augustine Webster OCart (c.1480–1535)

 UGUSTINE STUDIED AT Cambridge, became a member of the Carthusian community at Sheen and later was made prior of the Axholme Charterhouse. Though arrested and imprisoned in the Tower for refusing to swear to the Oath of Succession, Augustine was later released when he agreed to swear conditionally, that is insofar as it was lawful. Together with Robert Lawrence he met with John Houghton at the London Charterhouse to confer about the position to be taken by the Carthusians regarding the newly legislated Act of Supremacy. Thomas Cromwell met them and, when they refused to take the Oath of Supremacy without reservation, he imprisoned them in the Tower of London, where they were condemned to death for treason. The three monks, together with Richard Reynolds were executed at Tyburn, on 4 May 1535.

St Augustine, pray for us.

Richard Reynolds, OSsS (1490–1535)

 ICHARD WAS BORN in Devon. After taking a degree at Cambridge, he became a fellow of Corpus Christi College. In 1515 he joined the Bridgettine community at Syon Abbey. A renowned theologian, Richard was consulted by John Fisher and Thomas More on the subject of the King's proposed divorce, to which he was strongly opposed. Even though he was pressured to take the Oath of Supremacy, by which it was hoped that, as a person renowned for his learning and holiness, he would influence others to swear to it, he refused and was committed to the Tower. When tried in April 1535, he affirmed that, 'the King our sovereign Lord is not supreme head on earth of the Church of England'. He claimed that his view was held throughout Christendom, and even throughout the country by people who hesitated to make their views known publicly, as well as by the 'dead witness... of all the General Councils, [and] the holy doctors of the Church for the last fifteen hundred years'. He was sentenced to death and was executed at Tyburn, on 4 May 1535, with the three Carthusian priors who had refused to take the Oath.

On the scaffold he encouraged the others, promising them a 'heavenly supper' to follow their 'sharp breakfast taken patiently' for their Master's sake.

Collect (for the four martyrs)

Almighty ever-living God, who gave Saints John, Robert, Augustine, and Richard the grace of suffering for Christ, come, in your divine mercy, we pray, to the help of our own weakness, that, as your Saints did not hesitate to die for your sake, we, too, may live bravely in confessing you. Through our Lord Jesus Christ, your Son, who lives and reigns with you in the unity of the Holy Spirit, God, for ever and ever. Amen.

St Richard, pray for us.

4 May

Feast of the English Martyrs

Collect

Almighty God, who in our country raised up martyrs from every walk of life to vindicate the authority of your Church in teaching and worship, grant through their intercession, we pray, that all our people may be gathered once again to celebrate the same sacraments under the one shepherd, Jesus Christ your Son. Who lives and reigns with you in the unity of the Holy Spirit, God, for ever and ever. Amen.

English Martyrs, pray for us.

May 30

Luke Kirby (c.1548–1582)

Luke Kirby presents one of those distressing cases of a man who had prepared for years to serve God on the English mission but was abruptly denied the possibility. Born in Yorkshire, and educated most probably at Cambridge, he was ordained at Cambrai in 1577. He travelled to England with Edmund Campion, the future martyr, in 1580, and was arrested as he soon as he landed. Imprisoned at the Gatehouse prison in London, he was severely tortured over the following months, including with the scavenger's daughter. He was pressed to attend a Protestant church, but he refused. While in prison he managed to celebrate Mass with smuggled materials, of which a corporal survives at Stonyhurst. He was brought to trial with Edmund and seventeen other priests in 1581 on a charge of complicity in a plot to assassinate the Queen. Several of the accused, including Edmund, were found guilty through the evidence of false witnesses, and Luke was sentenced to be hanged, drawn, and quartered. He remained in prison for several months, at one stage writing,

> We look to suffer death very shortly, as already it is signified to us. Yet I much fear lest our unworthiness of that excellent perfection and crown of martyrdom should procure me a longer life.

The sentence was carried out on 30 May 1582. As he said at the Tyburn gallows, though he was condemned for alleged treason he was in fact being put to death for his religion.

He declared:

> My feet never did tread, my hands never did write, nor my wit ever invent any treason against her Majesty but always wished unto her as my own soul, desiring God to give her a prosperous reign and afterwards eternal happiness.

Collect (for one martyr)

Almighty and merciful God, who brought your martyr blessed Luke to overcome the torments of his passion, grant that we, who celebrate the day of his triumph, may remain invincible under your protection against the snares of the enemy. Through our Lord, Jesus Christ, your Son, who lives and reigns with you in the unity of the Holy Spirit, God, for ever and ever. Amen.

St Luke, pray for us.

21 JUNE

John Rigby (c.1570–1600)

 ORN IN LANCASHIRE of a family of recusants, John felt obliged to attend the
official church until he repented and
made contact with Fr John Gerard SJ, a prisoner
in the Clink prison, who reconciled him to the
Church. John confessed to being a Catholic when
appearing to give evidence upon a separate matter
before a magistrate, and was imprisoned in
Newgate until his trial, when he was found guilty
of having been reconciled by a Catholic priest and
sentenced to death. Upon hearing the sentence, he
declared to the judge,

> *Deo gratias,* all is but one death, and a
> fleabite, in comparison of that which it
> pleased my sweet Savior Jesus to suffer for
> my salvation. I humbly thank your lordship
> for your great pains; and I freely forgive
> your lordship and the poor jury, and all
> other persecutors whatsoever.

He had lived a short life but one that discovered
its true meaning, and he could not be deterred
from faithfulness to God. He was executed on 21
June 1600 at St Thomas Watterings, Old Kent
Road. Treated with exceptional savagery, John
was able to stand up after his hanging and was
held down with an attendant's foot on his throat
while he was being butchered. He managed to

speak the words during this ordeal, 'May God forgive you. Lord Jesus, receive my soul'.

Collect (for one martyr)

Almighty, ever-living God, by whose gift blessed John fought for righteousness's sake even until death, grant, we pray, through his intercession, that we may bear every adversity for the sake of your love and hasten with all our strength towards you who alone are life. Through our Lord, Jesus Christ, your Son, who lives and reigns with you in the unity of the Holy Spirit, God, for ever and ever. Amen.

St John, pray for us.

22 June[5]

John Fisher (1469–1535)

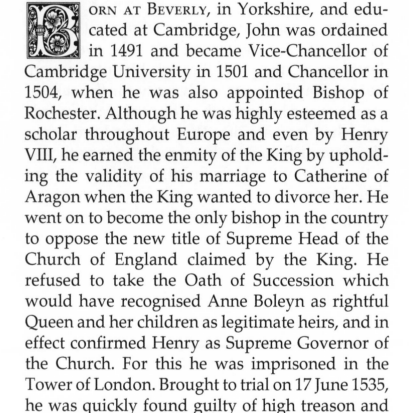

ORN AT BEVERLY, in Yorkshire, and educated at Cambridge, John was ordained
in 1491 and became Vice-Chancellor of
Cambridge University in 1501 and Chancellor in
1504, when he was also appointed Bishop of
Rochester. Although he was highly esteemed as a
scholar throughout Europe and even by Henry
VIII, he earned the enmity of the King by uphold-
ing the validity of his marriage to Catherine of
Aragon when the King wanted to divorce her. He
went on to become the only bishop in the country
to oppose the new title of Supreme Head of the
Church of England claimed by the King. He
refused to take the Oath of Succession which
would have recognised Anne Boleyn as rightful
Queen and her children as legitimate heirs, and in
effect confirmed Henry as Supreme Governor of
the Church. For this he was imprisoned in the
Tower of London. Brought to trial on 17 June 1535,
he was quickly found guilty of high treason and
sentenced to be hanged, drawn, and quartered,
but the public outcry was so great that this was
commuted by the King to beheading, and he was
executed five days later.

At the Tower of London scaffold he said,

---

5 St John Fisher and St Thomas More are included here
although they are not counted among the Forty Martyrs
as they had been canonised 35 years previously.

Christian people, I am come hither to die
for the faith of Christ's Catholic Church,
and I thank God hitherto my courage hath
served me well thereto, so that yet hitherto
I have not feared death; wherefore I desire
you help me and assist me with your
prayers, that at the very point and instant
of my death's stroke, and in the very
moment of my death, I then faint not in any
point of the Catholic Faith for fear; and I
pray God save the king and the realm...

St John, pray for us.

Thomas More (1478–1535)

ORN IN LONDON, and after receiving a
legal education at Lincoln's Inn, Thomas
lived at the London Charterhouse for four
years, 'religiously living there without vow', and
considered becoming a priest. In 1505, however,
he decided to marry and had four children before
his wife died in 1511. King Henry VIII recognised
his outstanding merits and promoted him swiftly
to high office, including as Speaker of the House
of Commons in 1523 and as Lord Chancellor in
succession to Cardinal Wolsey in 1529. When he
would not take the Oath of Succession, he was
imprisoned in the Tower of London, where he
remained for fifteen months. When the Act of
Supremacy came into effect in 1535 Thomas
refused to commit himself to it and was brought
to trial on 1 July 1535. Despite mounting a firm
defence based on multiple precedents, he was

found guilty of high treason and was sentenced to be hanged, drawn, and quartered. Thomas learned shortly afterwards that the King had commuted his sentence from disembowelment to beheading, in recognition of his years of service.

Coming to the Tower of London scaffold on 6 July, Thomas humorously remarked to the Master Lieutenant of the Tower, 'I pray you, Master Lieutenant, see me safe up and, for my coming down, I will shift for myself'. He told the bystanders to pray for him in this world, and that he would pray for them in the next. He affirmed that he died for the faith of the holy Catholic Church and added, 'the King's good servant, but God's first'.

Collect

O God, who in martyrdom have brought true faith to its highest expression, graciously grant that, strengthened through the intercession of Saints John Fisher and Thomas More, we may confirm by the witness of our life the faith we profess with our lips. Through our Lord, Jesus Christ, your Son, who lives and reigns with you in the unity of the Holy Spirit, God, for ever and ever. Amen.

St Thomas, pray for us.

23 JUNE

Thomas Garnet SJ (1575–1608)

 NEPHEW OF HENRY Garnet SJ, provincial of the Jesuits in England, Thomas was born in London and was ordained at Valladolid in 1599, before joining the Society of Jesus in 1604. He was arrested in 1605 under suspicion of being involved in the Gunpowder Plot and was confined to the Tower for several months. When it was established that he knew nothing of the Plot, he was exiled together with forty-six other priests in 1606. He soon returned to England but was quickly re-arrested after being betrayed by an apostate priest. He was sentenced to death for refusing to take the Oath of Supremacy and was executed at Tyburn, on 23 June 1608. Thomas is the protomartyr of St Omer, from which Stonyhurst College evolved.

At his trial he protested,

> The Prince issues a command: 'If any priest returns to England, let him be slain.' I have returned here and I consent to be put to death; thus I give my body to Caesar and my soul to God.

Collect (Jesuit Missal and Lectionary)

Almighty, eternal God, you chose from the people of England and Wales St Thomas to be made like Christ, who died to save the world. Listen to his prayers: strengthen the Church by the same faith and love that strengthened him, and bless it always with your gift of unity. Through our Lord, Jesus Christ, your Son, who lives and reigns with you in the unity of the Holy Spirit, God, for ever and ever. Amen.

St Thomas, pray for us.

27 JUNE

John Southworth (c.1584–1654)

 ORN IN LANCASHIRE, John went to Douai in 1613 to study for the priesthood and was ordained five years later before returning to England in 1619. For the next seven years he served as a priest in London, Brussels, and then in Lancashire, where he was arrested and condemned to death in 1628. He was released and banished through the intervention of Queen Henrietta Maria, the Catholic wife of King Charles I. However, he appears to have evaded exile and was able to work for the next twenty-five years in the Westminster area of London. After the plague broke out in 1636, he became known for his work with the future martyr Fr Henry Morse amongst the plague victims and recusants in the Westminster area. In and out of prison over the years, he none the less continued this work while on daily parole from prison. He was finally arrested in 1654 after a total of 35 years of missionary activity and, without the protection of the Queen since King Charles' execution, he was once again condemned to death and was hanged, drawn, and quartered at Tyburn, on 28 June 1654. His body was retrieved, stitched back together and, the only complete body of a Catholic martyr of the Penal Times, is now enshrined in Westminster Cathedral, in the district of London that he so dutifully served.

In a speech at the gallows, he declared,

My faith and my obedience to my superiors is all the treason charged against me; nay; I die for Christ's law, which no human law, by whomsoever made, ought to withstand or contradict ... To follow his holy doctrine and imitate his holy death I willingly suffer at present; this gallows I look on as his cross, which I gladly take to follow my dear Saviour.

Collect (for one martyr)

Almighty, ever-living God, by whose gift blessed John fought for righteousness's sake even until death, grant, we pray, through his intercession, that we may bear every adversity for the sake of your love and hasten with all our strength towards you who alone are life. Through our Lord, Jesus Christ, your Son, who lives and reigns with you in the unity of the Holy Spirit, God, for ever and ever. Amen.

St John, pray for us.

I JULY

Oliver Plunkett (1629–1681)[6]

LIVER WAS A scholarly Irishman who spent his early years as a priest and professor in Rome until, at the age of 40, he was appointed Archbishop of Armagh and sent back to Ireland to lead the pastoral work of the Church. He responded heroically to the challenge, since Ireland was woefully short of priests and the people were deprived of the sacraments. Hunted by the authorities, he travelled in disguise around the country building up the work of the Church through confirmations, establishing a school, and seeking to correct the behaviour of lax priests. The effectiveness of his work won him further enemies, and eventually false witness was brought against him, accusing him of fomenting rebellion against the English Crown and even of planning to organise a military invasion of Ireland by French soldiers. He was brought to trial in London on a series of totally unfounded charges of treasonous activity in Ireland. He was deprived of the opportunity to bring witnesses to his defence and was condemned to death for high treason. His execution, by being hanged, drawn, and quartered on 1 July 1681, was almost universally recognised

---

6 St Oliver Plunkett is included here, although he was Irish, because he was the last Catholic martyr to be executed at Tyburn and because, like several of the Forty Martyrs, he was brought to trial in the scare and persecution following the fictitious Titus Oates plot.

to have been completely unjustifiable, including by King Charles II himself, and this led to the suspension of capital punishment for priests from that time.

In his final speech, Oliver declared,

> [A]s ... holy Stephen did pray for those who stoned him to death; so do I, for those who, with perjuries, spill my innocent blood; I do heartily forgive them, and also the judges, who, by denying me sufficient time to bring my records and witnesses from Ireland, did expose my life to evident danger. I do also forgive all those who had a hand in bringing me from Ireland, to be tried here; where it was morally impossible for me to have a fair trial ... I beseech the All-powerful, that his Divine Majesty grant our king, queen, and the duke of York, and all the royal family, health, long life, and all prosperity in this world and in the next, everlasting felicity.

Collect

God our Father, you filled Saint Oliver with the spirit of fortitude, enabling him to feed your people with his word and to lay down his life for the faith; at his intercession keep us strong in that same faith and help us to proclaim it everywhere. Through our Lord, Jesus Christ, your Son, who lives and reigns with you in the unity of the Holy Spirit, God, for ever and ever. Amen.

St Oliver, pray for us.

12 July

John Jones OFM (1559–1598)

 Franciscan, born in Caernarvonshire, Wales, the details of whose early life are uncertain, John, serving as Franciscan provincial, ministered in the company of Fr John Gerard SJ in the London area from 1592 till 1597, when he was arrested, imprisoned, and tortured in the priest-hunter Topcliffe's house and after two years brought to trial for the treasonable offence of having been ordained abroad. He was convicted on his own admission that he was a priest, and was hanged, drawn, and quartered on 12 July 1598, at St Thomas Watterings, Old Kent Road, Southwark. Because the executioner had forgotten his rope, John used the hour he spent waiting on the scaffold to declare that treason was never in his mind.

At his trial, John had said,

> If this be a crime, I must own myself guilty;
> for I am a priest and came over into England
> to gain as many souls as I could to Christ.

Collect (for one martyr)

O God, by whose grace St John Jones combined a love of the Cross with a zeal for souls and gave his life for his priestly fidelity, grant us, through his intercession, constant fervour, and bring us to share in his reward. Through our Lord, Jesus Christ, your Son, who lives and reigns with you

in the unity of the Holy Spirit, God, for ever and
ever. Amen.

St John, pray for us.

19 July

John Plessington (1637–1679)

ORN IN LANCASHIRE and ordained under the assumed name of Scarisbrick in Spain in 1662, John ministered in Wales, at the Holywell shrine of St Frideswide, and then in the Wirral area where he pretended to be tutor to a family of children. Following the Titus Oates plot hoax, he was arrested in 1679 solely for being a priest and was hanged, drawn, and quartered on 19 July in Chester. He was one of more than twenty-three innocent Catholics whose lives were taken after they were accused of treason in the fictitious Popish Plot.

John's speech from the scaffold proclaimed his innocence of anything that could be called a crime:

> But I know it will be said that a priest ordained by authority derived from the See of Rome is, by the Law of the Nation, to die as a Traitor, but if that be so what must become of all the Clergymen of the Church of England, for the first Protestant Bishops had their Ordination from those of the Church of Rome, or not at all, as appears by their own writers so that Ordination comes derivatively from those now living.

He also declared,

> Nothing was laid to my charge except my priesthood … And I protest in the sight of God and the court of Heaven that I am

absolutely innocent of the plot so much discoursed of and abhor such bloody and damnable designs.... I had rather die than doubt any point of faith taught by our holy Mother, the Roman Catholic Church ... God bless the King ... and grant His Majesty a prosperous reign here and a crown of glory hereafter.

Collect (for one martyr)

Almighty and merciful God, who brought your martyr blessed John to overcome the torments of his passion, grant that we, who celebrate the day of his triumph, may remain invincible under your protection against the snares of the enemy. Through our Lord, Jesus Christ, your Son, who lives and reigns with you in the unity of the Holy Spirit, God, for ever and ever. Amen.

St John, pray for us.

22 JULY

Philip Evans SJ (1645–1679)

 ORN IN MONMOUTH, Wales, Philip joined the Jesuits in 1665. After being ordained in Belgium in 1675 he returned to Wales where he ministered for three years in the area of Abergavenny. He was arrested in 1678, following the fictitious Titus Oates plot. Although evidence against him proved hard to obtain, the jury at his trial was instructed to find him guilty through very questionable witnesses, and he was condemned to be hanged, drawn, and quartered. Being allowed considerable liberty while awaiting execution, Philip was playing tennis when he was informed that he was to die the following day; he went on to finish the game. He was executed on 22 July 1679.

Among his last words were, 'I die for religion and conscience's sake … I pray God bless and prosper the King'.

St Philip, pray for us.

22 JULY

John Lloyd (1640–1679)

 ORN IN BRECON, Wales, into a Catholic family, brother of a priest and of a nun, John attended the seminary in Valladolid and was ordained before returning to Wales in 1654, where he worked as a missionary priest for twenty-four years. Arrested in 1678 in Glamorgan, following the Titus Oates allegations, he was tried together with Philip Evans, and hanged, drawn, and quartered with Philip on 22 July 1679.

His last words were, 'I die for the Catholic and apostolic faith, according to these words in the Creed, I believe in the Holy, Catholic Church'.

Collect (for both saints)

Grant, we pray, O Lord, that we attain that fullness of faith which enabled your priests and martyrs Saints Philip and John to welcome death with constancy and joy. Through our Lord, Jesus Christ, your Son, who lives and reigns with you in the unity of the Holy Spirit, God, for ever and ever. Amen.

St John, pray for us.

24 JULY

John Boste (1543–1594)

OHN CAME FROM Westmoreland and studied at The Queen's College, Oxford University, before becoming a Fellow of the College and being ordained in the Anglican Church. At some stage he converted to the Catholic faith, was admitted to the English College at Rheims in 1580 and ordained in 1581. He returned to England immediately and worked very effectively for twelve years in the North, where he had a price on his head. Relentlessly pursued by the authorities, he was eventually arrested after celebrating Mass at a Catholic house near Durham in 1593. John boldly confessed to his priesthood and ministry. He was imprisoned and later transferred to the Tower of London where he was tortured on the rack and in other ways, but he disclosed nothing. When returned to Durham for trial, John denied all involvement in political affairs, saying that 'Our function is to invade souls and not to meddle with these temporal invasions'. He was nonetheless found guilty of treason and condemned to be hanged, drawn, and quartered. He was executed on 24 July 1594, after being forbidden to speak.

He just managed to say,

> I hope in God that if you will not suffer me to speak unto you in this world this my death will speak in your hearts that which I would have spoken.

Collect (for one martyr)

Almighty, ever-living God, by whose gift blessed
John fought for righteousness's sake even until
death, grant, we pray, through his intercession,
that we may bear every adversity for the sake of
your love and hasten with all our strength towards
you who alone are life. Through our Lord, Jesus
Christ, your Son, who lives and reigns with you
in the unity of the Holy Spirit, God, for ever and
ever. Amen.

St John, pray for us.

22 August

John Wall (1620–1579)

ORN IN LANCASHIRE, John Wall studied for the priesthood at Douai and was ordained in Rome, subsequently joining the Franciscan Order at Douai. In 1656 he returned to England and embarked on a twenty-three-year ministry based at Harvington Hall in Warwickshire before being arrested at the time of the fictitious Titus Oates plot and condemned as a Catholic priest. Although offered his freedom several times if he would take the Oath of Supremacy or renounce his religion, he refused and was confined to prison to await execution. He was hanged, drawn, and quartered at Worcester on 22 August 1579.

In a letter to his Franciscan Provincial, written the day before his death, he said,

> For the space of nine months I have been imprisoned as a child in the womb. And now that the nine months have elapsed, I hope that my Mother the Church will bring me forth to God, and that I shall enjoy light perpetual.

St John, pray for us.

22 August

John Kemble (1599–1679)

 OHN KEMBLE, ORIGINALLY from Hereford-shire, was ordained at Douai and returned immediately to England to serve a unique fifty-four years as an active priest in the Hereford and Monmouthshire areas. After being arrested in 1678, like John Wall following the Titus Oates allegations, he was condemned without any evidence against him except that he was a Catholic priest. At the age of eighty he died by hanging at Hereford, but only after enjoying a glass of wine and a pipe with the prison governor and the under-sheriff who came to summon him for his execution.

Among his last words he said,

> I die only for professing the old Roman Catholic religion, which was the religion that first made this kingdom Christian, and whosoever intends to be saved must die in the religion.

Collect (for both saints)

Grant a joyful outcome to our prayers, O Lord, so that we, who each year devoutly honour the day of the passion of the holy martyrs John Wall and John Kemble, may also imitate the constancy of their faith. Through our Lord, Jesus Christ, your Son, who lives and reigns with you in the unity of the Holy Spirit, God, for ever and ever. Amen.

St John, pray for us.

27 August

David Lewis SJ (1616–1679)

orn in Monmouthshire, Wales, David became a Catholic at the age of nineteen and soon afterwards entered the English College in Rome to study for the priesthood. Ordained in 1642, he joined the Jesuits two years later, returning to England in 1648 where he worked in Hereford for the next three decades in great danger from the parliamentary authorities of the Commonwealth. He was arrested under suspicion of being involved in the invented Titus Oates plot in 1678 but was tried and condemned simply for being a Catholic priest and was executed at Usk, on 27 August 1679. He was one of the last of the Forty Martyrs to meet this fate.

From the gallows, David said,

> If all the good things in this world were offered to me to renounce [my religion], all should not remove me one hair's breadth from my Roman Catholic faith... I was condemned for saying Mass, hearing confessions and administering the sacraments.

Collect

O God, who through the precious blood of your only Son have redeemed the human race, grant that, as we rejoice that your martyr Saint David was united to the sacrifice of your Son, your saving work may be accomplished in us, and we may become worthy to gather its fruit. Through our Lord, Jesus Christ, your Son, who lives and reigns with you in the unity of the Holy Spirit, God, for ever and ever. Amen.

St David, pray for us.

28 AUGUST

Edmund Arrowsmith SJ (1585–1628)

 ORN OF A family of recusants in Lancashire, Edmund (originally named Brian)
was a Douai priest on the mission in
Lancashire from 1613 for nine years before being
arrested in 1622, then released, and in 1624 became
a Jesuit. In 1628 he was betrayed, tried, and
condemned to be executed at Lancaster unless he
would renounce his faith. As he crossed Lancaster
Castle yard on his way to execution, he raised his
hand as a signal to the future martyr John Southworth to give him absolution. He was hanged,
drawn, and quartered on 28 August 1628.

When at the gallows he was asked, 'Will you
conform and lay hold of the King's mercy?' he
replied:

> The mercy I look for is in heaven… I freely
> and willingly offer to thee Sweet Jesus, this
> my death in satisfaction for my sins … I die
> for the love of thee, for our holy faith, for
> the support of the authority of thy vicar on
> earth, the successor of St Peter, the true
> head of the Catholic Church, which thou
> hast founded and established.

Collect (Jesuit Missal and Lectionary)

Almighty, eternal God, you chose from the people
of England and Wales St Edmund, and companions to be made like Christ, who died to save the

world. Listen to their prayers: strengthen the Church by the same faith and love that strengthened them, and bless it always with your gift of unity. Through our Lord, Jesus Christ, your Son, who lives and reigns with you in the unity of the Holy Spirit, God, for ever and ever. Amen.

St Edmund, pray for us.

30 AUGUST

Anne Line (c.1565–1601)

NNE, WHO WAS born in Essex, joined the Catholic Church at the age of nineteen with her younger brother William and they were disinherited by their Calvinist parents. She married young, but her husband, Roger, was arrested while attending Mass and was banished to Flanders, where he died some years later. Anne, who was left destitute, became housekeeper to Fr John Gerard SJ who maintained his house as a refuge for priests and where she carried out her duties so well despite very poor health that she was called Mrs Martha by the priests. In 1597, Fr Gerard was arrested and imprisoned in the Tower of London, from which he made a famous, and unique, escape. Her association with Fr Gerard obliged Anne to move to a new house but she kept up the work of assisting priests for which she dedicated herself by taking the three vows of poverty, chastity, and obedience. Her house was raided while a Mass was in progress in February 1601, and Anne was arrested, imprisoned at Newgate, and condemned to death for sheltering a priest, even though only priestly vestments were found, the priest having escaped. She was hanged at Tyburn, on 27 February 1601. Anne and her husband are believed to have been the subject of Shakespeare's allegorical poem *The Phoenix and the Turtle* in a Collection entitled *Love's Martyrs*.

At the gallows, she said,

> I am sentenced to die for harbouring a
> Catholic priest and so far am I from repent-
> ing of what I have done that I wish with all
> my soul that where I have entertained one
> I could have entertained a thousand.

St Anne, pray for us.

30 AUGUST

Margaret Ward (d. 1588)

 ARGARET, WHO WAS born in Cheshire, came to public notice in 1588 when she was arrested for helping a priest, William Watson, to escape from the Bridewell prison overlooking the Fleet river by smuggling a rope to him and securing a boat to await him in the river below the prison wall. In the year of the Armada, Catholic priests were the subject of fierce persecution, but Margaret resisted crippling torture to protect Fr Watson from discovery and refused to renounce her faith or to go against her conscience as the price of her freedom. She was hanged at Tyburn, on 30 August 1588, a day after her Old Bailey trial.

St Margaret, pray for us.

30 AUGUST

Margaret Clitherow (1553–1586)

N HER SHORT life of thirty-three years, and only the last twelve of them a Catholic, Margaret Clitherow played a significant part in the Catholic life of York, the city where she was born and where her Protestant husband held a leading position. In 1574 Margaret became reconciled to the Church and within two years her name figured on the list of local recusants. With the resources of a well-off family, she established a Mass centre, a hiding place for priests, and a small school in her house through which she brought support and comfort to the Catholic community. She spent several periods in prison as a recusant and was arrested a final time when a secret chapel in her house containing priests' vestments was disclosed by a boy servant. Because she refused to plead at her trial so as not to implicate her family, she was condemned to the legally approved, but immensely cruel *peine forte et dure* to be crushed to death under a wooden door with her arms outstretched and tied to stakes in the ground.[7] It is believed that she may have been pregnant. The Sheriff of York addressed her, saying 'Remember Mrs Clitherow, you die for treason'. But she replied 'No, Master Sheriff, I die

---

7   *Peine forte et dure* (from the French 'strong and hard punishment') in English law, was inflicted upon those who were accused of a felony and stood silent.

for the love of the Lord Jesus'. Under a weight of about 800 pounds, she moaned for a quarter of an hour until she died. Her execution took place on 25 March 1586. Margaret's courage and virtue were outstanding. She later became known as the 'Pearl of York'.

On her way to her execution, she is reported to have said, 'This way to heaven is as short as any other.'

Collect of the Feast (for the three martyrs)

Grant, Almighty God, to us who honour the fidelity in life and constancy in death of your holy martyrs, Saints Anne Line, Margaret Ward, and Margaret Clitherow, that they, who drew from you the strength to triumph, may likewise always obtain from you the grace of victory for us. Through our Lord, Jesus Christ, your Son, who lives and reigns with you in the unity of the Holy Spirit, God, for ever and ever. Amen.

St Margaret, pray for us.

10 SEPTEMBER

Edward (later Ambrose) Barlow OSB (1585–1641)

 ORN IN MANCHESTER and raised a Protestant, Edward was reconciled to the Church at twenty-two, and professed as a Benedictine monk with the name Ambrose at St Gregory's, Douai, in 1614. He returned to England as a priest three years later and worked very fruitfully for twenty-four years in north-west England. He was imprisoned and released several times, until finally in 1641 he was arrested, tried, and condemned after acknowledging that he was a priest and accounted thereby a traitor, though he was told he could be free if he promised not to seduce the people anymore. He replied,

> It will be easy to pledge my word to this since I am no seducer but a reducer of the people to the true and ancient religion. I have laboured to disabuse the minds of those who have fallen into error and I am resolved to continue until death to render this good office to these strayed souls.

Ambrose was hanged, drawn, and quartered at Lancaster on 10 September. He is greatly prized by the Benedictine Order, who count seven blesseds and three canonised saints, St John Roberts, St Alban Roe, and himself, among the martyrs.

Collect (for one martyr)

Almighty and merciful God, who brought your martyr blessed Ambrose to overcome the torments of his passion, grant that we, who celebrate the day of his triumph, may remain invincible under your protection against the snares of the enemy. Through our Lord, Jesus Christ, your Son, who lives and reigns with you in the unity of the Holy Spirit, God, for ever and ever. Amen.

St Ambrose, pray for us.

15 OCTOBER

Richard Gwyn (c.1537–1584)

ICHARD, BORN IN Montgomeryshire, Wales, studied at Cambridge and became a schoolmaster in what was then Flintshire, and later converted to the Catholic Church. Married with six children, he was threatened with imprisonment as a recusant and briefly conformed, but then moved home and opened another school. However, he came to the notice of the authorities in 1581 when he was arrested and forced to attend church. He was in chains and he rattled them so loudly that the preacher could not be heard. Richard was in fact known for his sense of humour. When placed in the stocks and pestered by Protestant ministers, one of whom who had a large, red nose claimed that the keys of the church were given no less to himself than to St Peter, Richard rejoined,

> There is this difference, namely, that whereas Peter received the keys to the Kingdom of Heaven, the keys you received were obviously those of the beer cellar.

He continued to be fined for recusancy until he could no longer pay, and yet was subjected to a huge fine of £140. He angered the judge by offering sixpence! In 1584 he was tried, accused of treason and, after the jury was threatened with dire consequences if they did not find him guilty, he was condemned to death for refusing to recognise the

Queen as head of the Church in England. He was hanged, drawn, and quartered on 15 October 1584, and is the protomartyr of Welsh recusants.

On the day of his execution, he remarked to one of a crowd of well-wishers, 'Weep not for me, for I do but pay the rent before the rent day.'

Collect (for one martyr)

Grant, O Lord, that the example of the life of service and suffering of your teacher and martyr, Saint Richard, may increase our love, inspire our service of the young, and heal the wounds dividing those who praise the name of Jesus Christ, your only Son, our Lord. Who lives and reigns with you in the unity of the Holy Spirit, God, for ever and ever. Amen.

St Richard, pray for us.

19 OCTOBER

Philip Howard (1557–1595)

 HILIP HOWARD, WHO was born in London to a family of high nobility, inherited his grandfather's title of Earl of Arundel. He was known in his youth as an ardent courtier and royal favourite of Queen Elizabeth I, but at twenty-seven he sought reconciliation to the Catholic faith and, after the failure of a plan to emigrate, was arrested and spent the remainder of his life as a prisoner in the Tower of London under sentence of death on spurious charges of treason. Once imprisoned, he was not allowed to see his wife again or the son that he had never even seen. For his loyalty to his family, he has been named patron of separated spouses.

Philip spent long hours in the Tower in remorseful prayer for his earlier life, in translating a major spiritual work from Latin and composing several poems, one of which laments the desecration of the shrine of Our Lady at Walsingham. Although he only managed to hear Mass a few times, he was devoted to Jesus and to Mary, and to the Rosary. He is especially remembered for having carved an inscription which is visible to this day on the wall of his cell in the Tower: "The more affliction for Christ in this world, the more glory with Christ in the next."

Among the Forty Martyrs, St Philip is unusual in that he did not actually shed his blood, but he was recognised as a martyr because he was wasted away by his ten-year imprisonment and died in agony, possibly poisoned, at the age of thirty-eight. Among his last recorded words, he spoke of forgiveness,

> And thus I will conclude with beseeching Almighty God the father of mercies, and God of all consolation, to grant peace unto his Church, charity and grace to mine enemies, salvation and felicity to the Queen and realm.

Philip deserves to be invoked as an intercessor for the reconciliation of Christians, for the restoration of the true faith in England, and for the reclaiming of the merits and prayers of all who suffered grievously or gave their lives for the faith during the Penal Times. Together with Our Lady, St Philip is co-patron of the Diocese of Arundel and Brighton.

Part of his poem—*In the Wracks of Walsingham*

> Bitter, bitter, O to behold
> The grass to grow
> Where the walls of Walsingham
> So stately did show.

> Such were the worth of Walsingham
> While she did stand,
> Such are the wracks as now do show
> Of that Holy Land.

> Level, level, with the ground
> The towers do lie,
> Which, with their golden glittering tops,
> Pierced once to the sky.

Collect (for one martyr)

Almighty, ever-living God, by whose gift blessed Philip fought for righteousness's sake even until death, grant, we pray, through his intercession, that we may bear every adversity for the sake of your love and hasten with all our strength towards you who alone are life. Through our Lord, Jesus Christ, your Son, who lives and reigns with you in the unity of the Holy Spirit, God, for ever and ever. Amen.

St Philip, pray for us.

25 OCTOBER

The Six Welsh Martyrs and their Companions

Collect of the Feast

Almighty God, who in our country raised up Martyrs from every walk of life to vindicate the authority of your Church in teaching and worship, grant at their intercession, we pray, that all our people may be gathered once again to celebrate the same Sacraments under the one Shepherd, Jesus Christ, your Son. Who lives and reigns with you in the unity of the Holy Spirit, God, for ever and ever. Amen.

The Six Welsh Martyrs, pray for us.

29 November

Cuthbert Mayne (c.1543–1577)

UTHBERT WAS EDUCATED in Barnstaple and at Oxford University, where he took the Oath of Supremacy and was ordained in the Church of England, becoming the chaplain of St John's College. However, he came under the influence of Edmund Campion and many other Catholics at the University and this led to his conversion to the Catholic faith about the year 1570. Encouraged by his Catholic friends, he crossed the Channel to Douai in 1573 as one of the earliest of the seminary students and was ordained a priest in 1575.

In April 1576 he returned to England where he posed as the steward at Francis Tregian's estate in Cornwall. On 8 June 1577, the high sheriff of Cornwall conducted a raid on Tregian's house during which Cuthbert was discovered. The officers found an *Agnus Dei* medallion and a number of documents, and he was taken into custody and later charged with high treason. At his trial he defended himself against six vague charges, but one of the judges directed the jury to return a verdict of guilty, stating that, 'where plain proofs were wanting, strong presumptions ought to take place'. The jury complied, finding Cuthbert guilty on all counts, and he was sentenced to be hanged, drawn, and quartered. He responded, '*Deo gratias*'. Before his execution at Launceston, Cuthbert

admitted that he was a priest. He died on 27
November 1577 and is recognised as the protomartyr of seminary priests.

When, at the gallows, he was offered his life in
return for a renunciation of his religion and an
acknowledgment of the supremacy of the Queen
as head of the church, he asked for a bible, made
the sign of the cross, kissed the holy book, and
declared, 'the Queen neither ever was, nor is, nor
ever shall be, the head of the church of England.'

Collect (for one martyr)

Almighty, ever-living God. By whose gift blessed
Cuthbert fought for righteousness's sake even
until death, grant, we pray, through his intercession, that we may bear every adversity for the sake
of your love and hasten with all our strength
towards you who alone are life. Through our Lord,
Jesus Christ, your Son, who lives and reigns with
you in the unity of the Holy Spirit, God, for ever
and ever. Amen.

St Cuthbert, pray for us.

1 December

Edmund Campion SJ (1540–1581)

 DMUND WAS BORN in London. He took the Oath of Supremacy and was ordained a deacon in the Church of England at Oxford. He attracted attention and admiration for his brilliance, including from the Queen, and could expect a successful career in the Church. However, influenced by Gregory Martin and other Catholics at the University, he became a Catholic and went first to Douai for training as a priest, then on to Rome and Prague to become a Jesuit. Returning to England in 1570, Edmund travelled to many parts of the country ministering to recusant Catholics, but at the same time made a name for himself by surreptitiously publishing the famous *Brag*, whose disparaging title was derived from the text of a defence of the faith addressed to Her Majesty's Privy Council, where he says,

> I would be loath to speak anything that might sound of any insolent brag or challenge, especially being now as a dead man to this world and willing to put my head under every man's foot, and to kiss the ground they tread upon. Yet I have such courage in avouching the majesty of Jesus my King, and such affiance in his gracious favour, and such assurance in my quarrel, and my evidence so impregnable, and because I know perfectly that no one Protestant, nor all the Protestants living ... can

maintain their doctrine in disputation. I am to sue most humbly and instantly for combat with all and every of them, and the most principal that may be found: protesting that in this trial the better furnished they come, the better welcome they shall be.[8]

Eventually captured by priest-hunters, after celebrating Mass at Lyford Grange in Berkshire, Edmund was offered ecclesiastical advancement if he conformed, but he refused and was tried and convicted of treason. He was tortured for information but revealed nothing of significance and was hanged, drawn, and quartered at Tyburn, on 1 December 1581, together with Ralph Sherwin and Alexander Bryant who were also condemned as priests.

In the spirit in which he had lived his faith, Edmund declared at the conclusion of their trial,

The only thing we have now to say is, that our religion do make us traitors, we are worthy to be condemned; but otherwise are, and have been, as good subjects as ever the Queen had. In condemning us you condemn all your own ancestors, all the ancient Bishops and Kings: all that was once the glory of England, the Island of Saints, and the most devoted child of the See of Peter. For what have we taught ... that they did not uniformly teach?

8   Campion also composed a book addressed to the academic world; entitled *Rationes decem* ('Ten Reasons'), the book gave arguments to prove the truth of Catholicism and the falsity of Protestantism, it was printed by the end of June 1581.

Collect (Jesuit Missal and Lectionary)

Almighty, eternal God, you chose from the people of England and Wales, St Edmund and companions to be made like Christ, who died to save the world. Listen to their prayers: strengthen the Church by the same faith and love that strengthened them, and bless it always with your gift of unity. Through our Lord, Jesus Christ, your Son, who lives and reigns with you in the unity of the Holy Spirit, God, for ever and ever. Amen.

St Edmund, pray for us.

1 December

Ralph Sherwin (1550–1581)

ORN IN DERBYSHIRE, Ralph studied very successfully at Oxford, becoming a fellow of Exeter College before being received into the Catholic Church and crossing to Douai for training as a priest. After ordination, he went to the English College in Rome in 1577, and in 1580 accompanied Edmund Campion to England. In a matter of a few months, he was arrested and imprisoned in the Marshalsea prison shackled in heavy chains. He commented on these in a letter to Fr Persons, 'I have on my feet some little bells that remind me, when I walk, who I am and to whom I belong. I have never heard sweeter harmony than this'. He was later sent to the Tower, where he was racked and pressured to conform to the Church of England. After a year he was tried with Edmund at Westminster Hall and condemned to be hanged, drawn, and quartered. At his trial he protested that, 'The plain reason for our standing here is religion, not treason'. His state of mind can be seen from the comment he made two days before his death, when with Edmund Campion he had been disputing with a Protestant minister, he looked up at the sun and said, 'Ah, Father Campion, I shall soon be above yonder fellow.' He was hanged, drawn, and quartered at Tyburn on 1 December 1581, and is recognised as the proto-martyr of the Venerable English College, in Rome.

When, at the gallows, he was urged to confess his treason, Ralph said,

> I have no occasion to lie, for so doing I should condemn my own soul; and although in this short time of mortal life I am to undergo the infamy and punishment of a traitor, I make no doubt of my future happiness, through Jesus Christ, in whose death, passion and blood I only trust.

Collect (for one martyr)

Almighty and merciful God, who brought your martyr blessed Ralph to overcome the torments of his passion, grant that we, who celebrate the day of his triumph, may remain invincible under your protection against the snares of the enemy. Through our Lord, Jesus Christ, your Son, who lives and reigns with you in the unity of the Holy Spirit, God, for ever and ever. Amen.

St Ralph, pray for us.

1 DECEMBER

Alexander Bryant SJ (1556–1581)

 LEXANDER'S LIFE FOLLOWED a similar pattern to that of Ralph Sherwin. He was born in Somerset, attended Oxford University, was reconciled to the Church in 1574 and went to Douai for priest training. Ordained in 1579, he returned to Somerset. He was arrested in 1581, when a group of priest-hunters found him while searching for Fr Robert Persons SJ. He was sent to the Tower, subjected to starvation and tortured on the rack, with the thumbscrew, with needles inserted under his nails, and with the scavenger's daughter. Despite the savagery with which he was repeatedly treated, Alexander refused to give any information about Fr Persons with whom he had been closely associated.[9] It is reported by Fr Persons that he laughed at his tormentors, and though nearly killed by the pain, said, 'Is this all you can do? If the rack is no more than this, let me have a hundred more for this cause.'

At his trial in Westminster Hall, on 21 November, he held a drawing of a cross which a Protestant minister present told him to throw away. He replied, 'Never will I do so, for I am a soldier of the Cross,

---

[9] On Alexander, the rack-master, Norton, used the inhuman threat that the martyr 'should be made a foot longer than God made him,' but later said that 'he was therewith nothing moved,' that he was 'racked more than any of the rest, yet he stood still with express refusal' to yield any information.

nor will I henceforth desert this standard until death'. When another minister snatched the cross from his hands, he said, 'You may tear it from my hands, but you cannot take it from my heart. Nay, I shall die for Him who first died on it for me.' He was found guilty of treason and was hanged, drawn, and quartered with Edmund Campion and Ralph Sherwin on 1 December 1581. He was just twenty-five. He had requested entry into the Jesuits before his death and is counted as belonging to the Society.

Collect (Jesuit Missal and Lectionary)

Almighty, eternal God, you chose from the people of England and Wales St Alexander and companions to be made like Christ, who died to save the world. Listen to their prayers: strengthen the Church by the same faith and love that strengthened them, and bless it always with your gift of unity. Through our Lord, Jesus Christ, your Son, who lives and reigns with you in the unity of the Holy Spirit, God, for ever and ever. Amen.

St Alexander, pray for us.

5 December

John Almond (c.1577–1612)

ORN NEAR LIVERPOOL, John was educated mainly in Ireland but went to the English College, Rome, at the age of twenty and was ordained four years later. He returned to England in 1602 and spent six years in active ministry before being arrested and imprisoned. He appears to have been released and to have worked in Staffordshire but was re-arrested in 1612 and sent to Newgate prison. He was convicted of being a priest, though this was never proved, and was executed at Tyburn, by being hanged, drawn, and quartered, on 5 December 1612. When questioned on the scaffold about how, as a priest, he could come into the country against the King's laws, he replied,

> Christ is the greater king. Laws made against Christ's laws are not binding. In case I were a priest, which has not been proved, I should have a commission from Christ who said, 'Go and teach all nations', to come and teach in England.

Collect (for one martyr)

Almighty, ever-living God, by whose gift blessed John fought for righteousness's sake even until death, grant, we pray, through his intercession, that we may bear every adversity for the sake of your love and hasten with all our strength towards you who alone are life. Through our Lord, Jesus Christ, your Son, who lives and reigns with you in the unity of the Holy Spirit, God, for ever and ever. Amen.

St John, pray for us.

10 December

Swithun Wells (1536–1591)

 withun Wells, a layman, was born in Hampshire. He lived a quiet life, managing a school in Wiltshire until he was obliged to give it up when suspected of Catholic sympathies and of protecting priests. He continued to assist priests in his London house and was several times arrested, and on one occasion interrogated about the Babington Plot. Two priests, Edmund Gennings and Polydore Plasden, were discovered by the notorious priest-hunter, Topcliffe, while celebrating Mass at Swithun's house on 28 November 1591. Although not present at the time, Swithun was later arrested and brought to trial. He was found guilty of harbouring priests and condemned to death. He was executed on gallows erected outside his house in Gray's Inn Lane, in London, on 10 December 1591, along with Edmund Gennings and Eustace White, who had been condemned for treason for their priesthood. Polydore Plasden and John Roberts, also condemned for their priesthood, were executed on the same day at Tyburn.

Topcliffe, the priest-hunter, who was present at all the executions, reproached Swithun, saying 'See what your priests have brought you to,' but Swithun replied, 'I am happy and thank God to have been so favoured to have so many and such saint-like priests under my roof.'

Collect

Almighty God, by your grace Saint Swithun taught his generation the power of Christ's passion. May we learn from him to place our hope in you alone and to remain faithful in every trial. We ask this through our Lord, Jesus Christ, your Son, who lives and reigns with you in the unity of the Holy Spirit, God, for ever and ever. Amen.

St Swithun, pray for us.

10 December

Edmund Gennings (1567–1591)

 orn in Staffordshire, Edmund became a Catholic in 1583, after serving as a page in a recusant household, and entered the English College in Rheims. He was ordained in 1590 and returned to England in the company of Polydore Plasden and other priests. In 1591 he met up again with Polydore Plasden and arranged to celebrate Mass with him the following day at the home of Swithun Wells. The Mass was interrupted by the arrival of the priest-hunter Topcliffe who arrested the two priests and took them to the Gatehouse prison. For celebrating Mass, the priests were condemned for treason. Edmund was hanged, drawn, and quartered while fully conscious on 10 December. At twenty-four, he was the youngest of the Forty Martyrs.

As he faced the gallows, Topcliffe told him to confess his treason, but Edmund replied,

> If to return to England a priest or to say Mass be popish treason, I here confess that I am a traitor; but I think not so and therefore I acknowledge myself guilty of those things, not with repentance, but with an open protestation of inward joy.

St Edmund, pray for us.

10 DECEMBER

Eustace White (1560–1591)

ORN IN LINCOLNSHIRE and raised a Protestant, Eustace converted in 1584 and two years later entered the English College in Rome. After ordination in 1588 he returned to England and ministered to Catholics in the West Country for three years. He was denounced by an acquaintance in 1591 and was arrested and imprisoned at the Bridewell prison in London. The Privy Council authorised his torture by Topcliffe, and he was racked seven times to try and make him reveal in what houses he had said Mass. He was tried with Edmund Gennings, Polydore Plasden, and Swithun Wells, and condemned to death for his priesthood. He was hanged, drawn, and quartered with them at Tyburn, on 10 December.

Eustace said to the assembled crowd,

> I thank God that it hath pleased him to bless my labours with this happy end, when I am now to die for my faith and my priesthood. Other treasons I have not committed.

St Eustace, pray for us.

10 DECEMBER

Polydore Plasden (1563–1591)

 ORN IN LONDON, Polydore (aka Oliver Palmer) attended Douai and Rheims Colleges and was ordained in Rome in 1586. He is believed to have ministered in Sussex and perhaps returned to Rheims with the threat to priests occasioned by the Spanish Armada in 1588. He returned to England in 1590 with Edmund Gennings but was soon arrested while celebrating Mass with Edmund at Swithun Wells' house in London. He was condemned for treason, though he defended himself from any such charge and professed loyalty to the Queen. He was hanged, but allowed to die before being drawn and quartered at Tyburn, on 10 December 1591.

Sir Walter Raleigh, who was present at the gallows when Polydore prayed for the Queen, asked him if he sincerely meant his prayers. Polydore replied, 'Yes, otherwise I could expect no salvation.'

Collect (for all three saints)

Grant a joyful outcome to our prayers, O Lord, so that we, who each year devoutly honour the day of the passion of the holy Martyrs, Edmund, Eustace and Polydore, may also imitate the constancy of their faith. Through our Lord, Jesus Christ, your Son, who lives and reigns with you in the unity of the Holy Spirit, God, for ever and ever. Amen.

St Polydore, pray for us.

10 December

John Roberts OSB (1576–1610)

 OHN WAS BORN in Merioneth, Wales, and educated at Oxford. He joined the Catholic Church in 1598 and entered the English College of St Alban, Valladolid. Together with a group of other students he joined the Benedictine Order and returned to England in 1602 where he worked devotedly amongst plague-victims. He had an active existence as a priest, being arrested four times, banished twice and escaping from prison once, all in seven years. While exiled, he helped found the Benedictine monastery of St Gregory at Douai (now Downside Abbey), of which he was the first prior. In 1610 he once more returned from exile to England but was quickly arrested while saying Mass. Accused at his trial at Newgate of being a 'seducer of the people', he replied, 'If I am, then our ancestors were deceived by St Augustine, the apostle of the English, who was sent here by the pope of Rome, St Gregory the Great, and who converted this country.' He was found guilty and condemned to death, and was hanged, drawn, and quartered at Tyburn, on 10 December 1610.

At the gallows he said,

> May it please you to hear that I stand now in this place ready to suffer the death to which I have been condemned, for no other reason but that, being a priest, I must die …

I have not committed any other crime but this one; whence it is clear that I die for the cause of religion, the religion, I say, which is the same as that brought here in days of old by St Augustine, Apostle of England, who was sent hither in the year 596 by the great Pope St Gregory ... He was a monk of the Order of St Benedict; I am one likewise ... It is for these reasons that I have been treated as a criminal and condemned to death.'

Collect

Preserve among your people, Lord, we pray, that faith which was handed down from your Apostles, assured by the authority of the Holy See, and professed by the blood of St John Roberts, your holy Martyr. Through our Lord, Jesus Christ, your Son, who lives and reigns with you in the unity of the Holy Spirit, God, for ever and ever. Amen.

St John, pray for us.

23 DECEMBER

John Stone (d.1539)

 NE OF THE first of the Forty Martyrs, and whose name headed the list of the English martyrs submitted to Rome for beatification, John was hanged, drawn, and quartered on 27 December 1539 in Canterbury. Though little is known about his life, other than that he had opposed King Henry's divorce, he was an Austin Friar who became known when Cromwell's Visitor, the suffragan Bishop of Dover, came to his community in Canterbury to dissolve the Friary. John was the only member of the community to refuse to take the Oath of Supremacy though all his confreres were expelled from the Friary without compensation. After spending a year in prison in London, John was sent to Canterbury to be tried under the Treason Act. He was swiftly convicted and subjected to a very public execution as a warning to others.

It is reported that on the scaffold John declared, 'I close my apostolate in my blood. In my death I shall find life, for I die for a holy cause, the defence of the Church of God.'

Collect (for one martyr)

Almighty, ever-living God, by whose gift blessed John fought for righteousness's sake even until death, grant, we pray, through his intercession, that we may bear every adversity for the sake of your love and hasten with all our strength towards you who alone are life. Through our Lord, Jesus Christ, your Son, who lives and reigns with you in the unity of the Holy Spirit, God, for ever and ever. Amen.

St John, pray for us.

EPILOGUE

 HILE MANY OF the Catholic martyrs of the Penal Times have a local following or have been honoured in particular shrines, it is to be regretted that most are unknown to the majority of the faithful. The same is of course true of very many canonised saints, but the difference is that these martyrs are a significant part of the history of the Church in the country that many of them loved and for which they prayed in the final moments of their lives. Do we not need to recapture the evident supernatural perspective of these men and women, their sense of the supreme importance of the Creator's love and the sacrifice of his Son for the sake of the eternal life of those who believe in him?

What do the martyrs bring us that we need? Spiritually, they can teach us about courage, perseverance, and suffering as 'co-redeemers', in the sense that their suffering is a sharing in the suffering of Christ, the one Redeemer, and they can lend their support to the Catholic Church in our times. We can ask them to pray for the raising up of a new generation of saints who will bear courageous witness to the faith in today's secular society, or for all in leadership positions in the Church that they may be faithful and resolute in affirming authentic liturgy, doctrine, and morals. They can also be signs of hope, as evidenced by the Masses at the Martyrs' Shrine in Tyburn Convent, the honouring of St John Southworth buried at Westminster Cathedral, the commemoration of the Douai priest martyrs and St Thomas More at Allen Hall seminary in London, or the devotion to St Philip Howard as co-patron of the Diocese of Arundel and Brighton.

Christian unity remains a priority for the Church because of Christ's prayer that we should all be one as he and the Father are one. The century and a half of persecution of the Catholic Church cannot be forgotten, but with God's grace it can be forgiven, and enlisting the martyrs' intercession for Church unity would be an act of trust in their holiness and a spur for today's Christians, Catholics, Anglicans, and Protestants, to respond to the divine desire for our reconciliation.

Finally, in the wider world, Catholics today undoubtedly share with the martyrs the status of *strangers and nomads*, and this may be the destiny of the Church in the modern age, but we nevertheless have a responsibility to endeavour to evangelise the culture of our time. We may also have to suffer for the Church as did the Catholic martyrs of the Reformation times. Perhaps the cultural shift occasioned by the Covid pandemic will come to be seen as an opportunity for a re-birth and a time of purification needed not only by the Church but by the whole world.

APPENDIX

LIST OF THE BEATIFIED MARTYRS

(with date of death, where known)

Beatified by Pope Leo XIII, 29 December 1886

Thomas Abel, priest, 30 July 1540
Richard Bere, Carthusian monk, 9 August 1537
Thomas Cottam, Jesuit priest, 30 May 1582
John Davy, Carthusian, 8 June 1537
William Exmew, Carthusian monk, 19 June 1535
John Felton, layman, 8 August 1570
Richard Fetherston, Archdeacon, 30 July 1540
William Filby, 30 May 1582
Thomas Ford, 28 May 1582
John Forest, Franciscan friar, 22 May 1538
German Gardiner, layman, 7 March 1544
Thomas Green, Carthusian, 10 June 1537
William Greenwood, Carthusian brother, 6 June 1537
John Haile (or Hale), priest, 4 May 1535
Everard Hanse, priest, 1581
William Hart, priest, 1583
William Horne, Carthusian lay brother, 4 August 1540

Robert Johnson, priest, 1582
Thomas Johnson, Carthusian, 20 September 1537
Richard Kirkman, priest, 1582
William Lacy (or Lacey), priest, 22 August 1582
John Larke, priest, 7 March 1544
Humphrey Middlemore, Carthusian monk, 19 June 1535
John Nelson, priest, 1577
Sebastian Newdigate, Carthusian monk, 19 June 1535
Walter Pierson, Carthusian brother, 10 June 1537
Thomas Plumtree, priest, 1570
Edward Powell, 30 July 1540
Thomas Redyng, Carthusian, 16 June 1537
Lawrence Richardson (aka Lawrence Johnson), 30 May 1582
John Rochester, Carthusian monk, 11 May 1537
Margaret Pole, Countess of Salisbury, 27 May 1541
Robert Salt, Carthusian brother, 9 June 1537
Thomas Scryven, Carthusian, 15 June 1537
John Shert, priest, 1582
Thomas Sherwood, layman, 1579
John Story, Chancellor to Bishop Bonner, 1571
Richard Thirkeld, priest, 1583
James Tompson, priest, York, 1582
James Walworth, Carthusian monk, 11 May 1537
Thomas Woodhouse, priest, 1573

Beatified by Pope Leo XIII, 13 May 1895

John Beche (or Thomas Marshall), Abbot of Colchester, 1 December 1539

John Eynon, priest, 14 November 1539

Hugh Faringdon, Abbot of Reading, 14 November 1539

Adrian Fortescue, Knight of St John of Jerusalem, 9 July 1539

Roger James, Benedictine, 15 November 1539

Thomas Percy, Earl of Northumberland, 1572— Leader of the Rising of the North

John Rugg (or Rugge), Benedictine monk, 15 November 1539

John Thorne, Benedictine monk, 15 November 1539

Richard Whiting, Abbot of Glastonbury, 15 November 1539

Beatified by Pope Pius XI, 15 December 1929

Henry Abbot, layman, 4 July 1597
John Amias, priest, 16 March 1589
Robert Anderton, priest, 25 April 1586
William Andleby, priest, 4 July 1597
Ralph Ashley, Jesuit priest, 7 April 1607
Thomas Aufield, priest, 6 July 1585
Christopher Bales, priest, 4 March 1590
Mark Barkworth, Benedictine, 27 February 1601
William Barrow, aka William Harcourt, 20 June 1679
James Bell, priest, 1584
James Bird (or Byrd or Beard), layman, 25 March 1592
John Bodey, priest, 2 November 1583
Thomas Bosgrave, layman, 4 July 1594
William Browne, layman, 5 September 1605
Christopher Buxton, priest, died Canterbury, 1 October 1588
Edward Campion (also known as Gerard Edwards), 1 October 1588
John Carey, Dublin born lay helper of John Cornelius SJ, 4 July 1594
Edmund Catherick, priest, 1642
James Claxton (Clarkson), priest, 1588
Edward Colman (or Coleman), layman, 1678
Ralph Corbie, Jesuit, 7 September 1644
John Cornelius, Jesuit priest, 4 July 1594
Ralph Crockett, priest, 1 October 1588
Robert Dalby, priest, York, 16 March 1589
William Dean, priest, 28 August 1588

Francis Dicconson, priest, 1590
Roger Dicconson, priest, 7 July 1591
James Duckett, layman, 1601
John Duckett, priest, 1644
Thomas Felton, Franciscan, 1588
James Fenn, priest, 1584
John Fenwick, Jesuit priest, 1679
John Finch, 1584
William Freeman, priest, 1595
Edward Fulthrop, layman, 1597
John Gavan, Jesuit priest, 1679
Miles Gerard, priest, 1590
George Gervase, Benedictine, 1608
David Gonson (or Gunston), layman, 12 July 1541
Hugh Green, priest, 1642
John Grove, layman, 24 January 1679
William Gunter, priest, 1588
William Harrington, priest, 1594
William Hartley, priest, 1588
Thomas Hemerford, priest, 1584
Richard Herst (Hurst), layman, 29 August 1628
John Hewitt (aka Weldon, aka Savell), priest, 1588
Sydney Hodgson, layman, 10 December 1591
Thomas Holford, priest, 1588
Thomas Holland, priest, 12 December 1642
Laurence Humphreys (or Humphrey), layman, 1591
John Ingram, priest, 1594
John Ireland, priest, 7 March 1544
William Ireland, Jesuit priest, 1679
Edward James, priest, 1588
Edward Jones, priest, 1590

Brian Lacey, layman, 1591
Richard Langhorne, layman, 1679
Richard Langley, layman, 1586
Richard Leigh, priest, 1588
John Lockwood, priest, 1642
William Marsden, priest, 25 April 1586
Richard Martin, layman, 30 August 1588
John Mason, layman, 1591
Thomas Maxfield, priest, 1616
Anthony Middleton, priest, 1590
Ralph Milner, layman, 7 July 1591
Hugh More, layman, 28 August 1588
Robert Morton, priest, 1588
John Munden, priest, 1584
George Napper (aka Napier), priest, 1610
John Nutter, priest, 1584
Edward Oldcorne, Jesuit priest, 1606
Francis Page, Jesuit, 1602
William Patenson, priest, 1592
John Pibush, priest, 1601
Thomas Pickering, Benedictine, 1679
Philip Powell, Benedictine, 1646
Alexander Rawlins, priest, 1595
Thomas Reynolds, priest, 21 January 1642
William Richardson, priest, 1603
John Robinson, priest, 1 October 1588
John Roche, layman, 1588
Patrick Salmon, layman, 4 July 1594
Maurus Scott (William Scot) 1612
Edward Shelley, 30 August 1588
John Slade, layman, 1583
Richard Smith, (aka Richard Newport), priest, 1612

Thomas Somers, priest, 1610
John Speed, layman, 4 February 1594
William Howard, 1st Viscount Stafford, layman, 29 December 1680
Edward Stransham, priest, 1586
Robert Sutton, layman, 5 October 1588
George Swallowell, layman, 26 July 1594
Thomas Thwing, priest, 1679
Thomas Tunstall, priest, 1616
Anthony Turner, Jesuit, 1679
Thomas Warcop, layman, 4 July 1597
William Ward, priest, 1641
Edward Waterson, priest, 1593
Robert Watkinson, priest, 1602
William Way (aka May or Flower), priest, 1588
Thomas Welbourne, layman, 1 August 1605
Thomas Whitbread, Jesuit, 1679
Robert Widmerpool, layman, 1 October 1588
Robert Wilcox, priest, 1 October 1588
Peter Wright, Jesuit, 1651

Beatified by Pope St John Paul II, 22 November 1987

John Adams, priest, 8 October 1586
Thomas Atkinson, priest, 1616
Edward Bamber, priest, 1646
George Beesley, priest, 5 July 1591
Arthur Bell, Franciscan priest, 1643
Thomas Belson, layman, 5 July 1589
Robert Bickerdike, layman, 23 July 1586
Alexander Blake, layman, 4 March 1590
Marmaduke Bowes, layman, 26 November 1585
John Britton (aka Bretton), layman, 1 April 1598
Thomas Bullaker, Franciscan priest, 1642
Edward Burden, priest, 1588
Roger Cadwallador, priest, 1610
William Carter, layman, 11 January 1584
Alexander Crow, priest, 30 November 1587
William Davies, priest, 27 July 1593
Robert Dibdale, priest, 8 October 1586
George Douglas, priest, 1587
Robert Drury, priest, 1607
Edmund Duke, priest, 27 May 1590
George Errington, layman, 1596
Roger Filcock, priest, 1601
John Finglow (Fingley), priest, 8 August 1586
Matthew Flathers, priest, 1608
Richard Flower, layman, 1588
Nicholas Garlick, priest, 1588
William Gibson, layman, 1596
Ralph Grimston, layman, 1598
Robert Grissold, layman, 1604

John Hambley, priest, 1587
Robert Hardesty, layman, 1589
George Haydock, priest, 12 February 1584
Henry Heath, Franciscan priest, 1643
Richard Hill, priest, 27 May 1590
John Hogg, priest, 27 May 1590
Richard Holiday, priest, 27 May 1590
Nicholas Horner, layman, 4 March 1590
Thomas Hunt, priest, 1600
Thurstan Hunt, priest, 1601
Francis Ingleby, priest, 3 June 1586
William Knight, layman, 1596
Joseph Lambton, priest, 24 July 1592
William Lampley, layman, 1588
John Lowe, priest, 8 October 1586
Robert Ludlam, priest, 1588
Charles Mahoney (aka Meehan), Franciscan priest,
1679
Robert Middleton, priest, March 1601
George Nichols, priest, 1589
John Norton, layman, 1600
Robert Nutter, priest, 1600
Edward Osbaldeston, priest, 1594
Antony Page, priest, 1593
Thomas Palasor, priest, 1600
William Pike, layman, 1591
Thomas Pilchard, priest, 21 March 1587
Thomas Pormort, priest, 20 February 1592
Nicholas Postgate, priest, 1679
Humphrey Pritchard, layman, 1589
Christopher Robinson, priest, 1597
Stephen Rowsham, priest, 1587

John Sandys, priest, 11 August 1586
Montford Scott, priest, 1591
Richard Sergeant, priest, 2 April 1586
Richard Simpson, priest, 1588
Peter Snow, priest, 1598
William Southerne, priest, 1618
William Spenser, priest, 1589
Thomas Sprott, priest, 1600
John Sugar, priest, 1604
Robert Sutton, priest, 1587
Edmund Sykes, priest, 23 March 1587
John Talbot, layman, 1600
Hugh Taylor, priest, 25 November 1585
William Thomson, priest, 20 April 1586
Robert Thorpe, priest, 1591
John Thulis, priest, 18 Mar 1616
Edward Thwing, priest, 26 July 1600
Thomas Watkinson, layman, 31 May 1591
Henry Webley, 28 August 1588
Christopher Wharton, priest, 1600
Thomas Whitaker, priest, 1646
John Woodcock, Franciscan priest, 7 August 1646
Nicholas Woodfen, priest, 21 January 1586
Roger Wrenno, layman, 1616
Richard Yaxley, priest, 1589

BIBLIOGRAPHY

There is a considerable fugitive literature on the martyrs, mainly in pamphlet form and most of it highly derivative. The works selected below represent the more substantial or most researched publications that I have used.

Brennan, M. *Martyrs of the English Reformation* (Kansas: Angelus Press, 1991).

Camm, Dom Bede (ed.) *Lives of The English Martyrs* (vol. II) (London: Longman, Green and Co., 1914).

Caraman, P. *Henry Garnet 1555–1605 and the Gunpowder Plot* (London: Longman, Green & Co., 1964).

—— *Henry Morse: Priest of the Plague and Martyr of England* (London: Fontana, 1952).

Catholic National Shrine and Basilica of Our Lady, *Litany of the Saints and Martyrs of England and Wales* (Walsingham, 2020).

Challoner, R. *Memoirs of Missionary Priests and other Catholics of both Sexes that have suffered Death on Religious Accounts from the Year 1577 to 1684*, vols 1 and 2 (Manchester: Haydock, 1803)

Duffy, E. *The Stripping of the Altars: Traditional Religion in England c.1400–c.1580* (Newhaven: Yale University Press, 1992).

Farmer, D. H. (ed.) *The Oxford Dictionary of Saints* (Oxford: OUP.1992).

Gerard, J. *The Autobiography of a Hunted Priest* (San Francisco: Ignatius Press, 2012).

Plunkett, D. *The Noble Martyr: A Spiritual Biography of St Philip Howard* (Leominster: Gracewing, 2019).

Pullan, M. *The Lives and Times of the Forty Martyrs of England and Wales 1535–1680* (New Generation Publishing, 2013).

Saward, J. et al. (eds) *Firmly I Believe and Truly: The Spiritual Tradition of Catholic England* (Oxford: Oxford University Press, 2011).

Waugh, E. *Edmund Campion, Jesuit and Martyr* (London: Penguin, 2012).

Lightning Source UK Ltd.
Milton Keynes UK
UKHW010340011121
393173UK00004B/25